# ACTIVITY BASED MANAGEMENT:
# IMPROVING PROCESSES AND PROFITABILITY

# ACTIVITY BASED MANAGEMENT: IMPROVING PROCESSES AND PROFITABILITY

Brian Plowman

Gower

SVA (Shareholder Value Added), EVA (Economic Value Added) and Windows NT are all registered trademarks.

Published by
Gower Publishing Limited
Gower House
Croft Road
Aldershot
Hampshire GU11 3HR
England

Gower Publishing Company
131 Main Street
Burlington VT 05401-5600 USA


Brian Plowman has asserted his right under the Copyright, Designs and Patent Act 1998 to be identified as the author of this work.


British Library Cataloguing in Publication Data
Plowman, Brian
   Activity based management : improving processes and
   profitability
   1. Activity-based costing    2. Managerial accounting
   I. Title
   658.1'511


   ISBN 0 566 08145 8


Library of Congress Cataloging-in-Publication Data
Plowman, Brian.
    Activity based management : improving processes and profitability/Brian Plowman.
      p.  cm.
    Includes index.
    ISBN 0-566-08145-8  (hardback)
    1. Activity-based costing.   2. Management.    I. Title

   HF5686.C8 P5934   2001
   658.15'54–dc21                                                                2001033410



Typeset in Century Old Style by IML Typographers, Birkenhead and printed in Great Britain by TJ International Ltd, Padstow, Cornwall.

# Contents

**Part III    Case Studies**

# List of figures and tables

■

## FIGURES

# TABLES

# Foreword

The battle to sustain and increase corporate profitability grows ever more arduous in most sectors of the economy. Margins are caught in a pincer movement by, on the one hand, the steady improvement in competition and, on the other, the increasing awareness of customers. Things are ever changing. Now we see more businesses moving into the e-world. This has provided major opportunities to increase business, but comes at a price. From aware customers comes the demand for lower prices; a share of the lower costs assumed to come from doing e-business.

There is no room for complacency. We need to grasp every opportunity not only to be ever more effective at what we do, but also to be truly competitive, winning more market share of the customers both nationally and globally. For success, a full understanding of costs and cost structures is necessary. Conventional accounting and management reporting throw little light on the real cost dynamics in a business. As a result we are not in control of profitability at a level of detail that supports substantive decision-making.

Activity Based Management (ABM) is an approach that has now come of age. ABM is not a technique; it is about management. ABM needs to be understood and implemented by all functions so its power can be unleashed and the benefits obtained.

Over time, ABM has evolved considerably and is now being applied in manufacturing, service companies, utilities, logistics, telecommunications, government bodies and many other sectors. With ABM, businesses can make dramatic improvements in measuring product and process costs, and more importantly customer profitability.

Brian Plowman has created a reader-friendly, comprehensive narrative covering the key aspects of the theory and practice of ABM. Executives and managers in all functions in all types of organizations, as well as students, will appreciate this book's practical and down-to-earth approach with many practical illustrations drawn from experience.

As well as step-by-step guidance on basic principles, comparisons with traditional methods, definitions of processes, activities, cost-drivers, data collection techniques and implementation steps, this book uses numerous detailed examples drawn from practice to build a logical picture of how to obtain the benefits of ABM.

On its own, ABM help will change management decision-making. By understanding how ABM also supports other profit improvement initiatives such as Business Process Reengineering, Shareholder Value Added and Customer Relationship Management, managers will learn how they can have the best possible toolkit to help put the business firmly on the road to leaps in profitability.

This book should be required reading for anyone within an organization who has the responsibility to grow their business profitably.

Professor Michael Bromwich
CIMA Professor of Accounting
Department of Accounting and Finance
London School of Economics

# 1 Introduction

## CUSTOMERS

We know that customers are important to us. But even when we achieve the right orientation towards customers, we know, instinctively, that some customers are more profitable than others. We also know that some are probably loss-making. For some businesses, this doesn't matter much. If margins are good enough, for whatever reason (a captive market, or a patent, or regulatory protection, and so on), overall profitability is sufficient. But few businesses have that luxury.

We may also have some idea of which customers are the least profitable, and which are the most profitable. A walk around the business listening to anecdotes in different departments will tell us which customers are demanding of time and effort and cost: these are the customers who order unpredictably, amend their orders, change specifications at the last minute, delay payment, require special deliveries, and so on. Every department will have its own, separate experiences of customer behaviour. Nobody will have the whole picture. So anecdotal evidence will pick up the extremes – the 'worst' and the 'best' customers. What about the others?

Customer profitability is a black hole in most managers' understanding of their business. Identifying customer revenue is easy: it's shown in the sales ledger. Identifying what individual customers cost – so we can understand whether or not they are profitable – is difficult. In a world in which competition, and often regulation, put increasing pressure on margins, it is vital to understand both product and customer profitability.

As if competition were not enough to put pressure on margins, electronic commerce (e-commerce) promises lower unit costs and creates customer expectations of lower prices.

# THE TWENTY-FIRST CENTURY IS ELECTRONIC

Technology advances, rapidly. Now companies can record and process all available facts about their customers, logging their every purchase and preference, storing details of each transaction and interaction – be it through call-centre, e-mail or post. If customers visit a Web site, a company can know their every key-stroke and click. And it is possible to analyse the information to death. If the marketeers have got it right, they can predict customers' every need and anticipate their every whim. Web routings, pages and menus can be programmed to reflect the history of the customer and the actions taken on-line. Just like good salespeople, but at a fraction of the cost, they can package and price offers not to target a niche, but an individual. Welcome to the world of one-to-one marketing.

Buying decisions become quicker and easier because customers are propositioned only with what they find attractive, in a process they judge convenient, safe and painless. Soon customers will have forgotten how on earth they managed in the scrum of mass marketing when they had to do the donkey work. And on top of all this, sales costs plummet as the need for expensive salespeople and high street outlets, and for slow-turning showroom stock, disappears.

It is enough to make a chief executive salivate. So where's the catch? In fact there are two. The first is that all the competitors will be doing the same thing. Unless a company can take an early lead and then defend its additional market share, or unless the concoction of technology and marketing in this brave new world increases the size of the total market, the only hope is to do it better than the competitors – which is what organizations try to do every day. The second catch is that all the hyperbole about e-commerce usually has a special message to the customer. It says 'lower prices'. After all, why do we put up with the DIY purgatory of supermarket shopping if it isn't for cheaper groceries? Instead of being able to pass on to the customer the cost of all the expensive technical wizardry, companies will find that margins are squeezed even more!

So is electronic commerce merely a development in which companies are forced to participate as a defensive measure, to the benefit only of customers and systems suppliers? Not necessarily.

# THE MISSING DIMENSION

Customer Relationship Management (CRM) is aimed at capturing information that will allow companies to create the circumstances in which customers will buy. It maximizes the attractiveness of the offer and the convenience of the sale by matching the selling process to the customer. But in making the match, it risks driving hidden costs into the business, be it by shortening delivery lead times, by encouraging complex product variants, by offering high levels of personal service, or by attracting customers who trigger excessive costs. It's as if CRM provides a more extravagant, indulgent courtship display, but pays no attention to the slog of making the marriage work in the long term.

It is not enough for companies to use CRM to anticipate every interaction the customer might have with the business, before, during and after the sale. They must understand the costs driven by those interactions.

When the dust has settled on the expensive new e-commerce implementation and its bewildering array of 'bundled' products and services, customer profitability becomes the missing dimension, hidden deep in the business. Understanding all the costs that are driven by customer behaviours, some of them maddeningly cryptic, is vital to designing the processes and setting the prices that companies offer. Otherwise, they risk making customer promises they cannot profitably fulfil.

## CAN ALL CUSTOMERS BE KINGS?

Not all customers are created equal in the sight of the supplier. They behave differently from one another and have a variety of characteristics, so they generate different costs and margins. Some are highly profitable, others are spectacularly unprofitable, and many lie in between. Often, a small, anonymous group of customers contributes the major share of profits, while an equally invisible segment erodes it.

A clear understanding of customer profitability allows a business to differentiate the level of service it provides to various customer segments according to their needs and their value to the company. For example, it may offer individual attention to prized customers in the form of dedicated telephone lines, free delivery, incentive pricing or customized products. At the same time, it might choose to reduce service to unprofitable customers – or to increase prices – even at the risk of losing them. A comprehensive view of the costs that customers drive allows a business to refine its processes and policies and focus its resources where they will have the greatest effect on profits: cementing customer relationships; avoiding excessive costs; matching prices to the service given.

In many sectors, the customer continues to provide revenue and to drive costs well after the initial sale, through after-sales service, repeat purchasing or general administration. All these costs, as well as the revenues, need to be identified and analysed to ensure that the initial terms are profitable and that the customer segments a company targets have a high probability of being profitable over the lifetime of the relationship.

An added benefit of customer profitability analysis is that it highlights the costs of poorly designed internal processes. As the true costs of processes emerge, managers can sense which costs are suspiciously high. This triggers a cycle of further investigation, problem identification and process improvement, thereby correcting profit-harming defects that would otherwise continue undetected.

## ACTIVITY BASED MANAGEMENT

Activity Based Management (ABM) enables managers to understand product and customer profitability, the cost of business processes, and how to improve them. Since conventional management accounts and standard costing systems do not provide this information, it is perhaps surprising that ABM is not more widely used. Unlike many management techniques, research shows that 80 per cent of companies that have employed activity-based techniques found them to be successful.

Why? Activities consume resources – people, materials and equipment – and this consumption can be measured. Activities are triggered by events, which can be counted, or decisions, which can be reviewed. Activities produce outputs – products and services, which can be counted and measured. Activities can be undertaken by different methods, which will vary the unit cost. Activities are linked together to form business processes. Understanding what activities are, what they cost, what drives them, what they produce, how they are done and how they are linked together is useful.

We have understood manufacturing activities in this way for years. We measure the consumption of direct labour and materials in making products. On average, however, direct labour, materials and components account for around two-thirds of total costs in manufacturing businesses. The other, unmeasured, third is overhead activities and costs. In service industries, the ratio is the other way round – the unmeasured 'overhead' accounts for two-thirds or more of costs.

Overhead costs are the black hole in conventional management information systems. ABM shines light into the hole. Knowledge of a business at the level of activities is the basic building block upon which new understanding can be built of where profits are being made and where they are being eroded.

By making visible what was previously invisible, ABM throws a spotlight on those aspects of a business where action can directly improve business performance. Because it deals with 'financial numbers', ABM is often seen as the preserve of the Finance function. In fact, its real strength lies in providing genuinely useful information for all functions in an organization. Managers throughout the business need the right information to understand and address two key issues:

- how the company can position itself better in the market – for which accurate product and customer profitability information is vital

- how it can improve its internal capability and lower unit costs – for this, it needs to understand and change the procedures, systems and processes that create products and deliver services to customers.

Most organizations are complex. Building an ABM model of a business requires a structured approach and the dedication of a team to achieve a result in a reasonable timescale. But building a model is only the start. Embedding ABM into the business means giving managers not only a new understanding of what drives costs, but the means to measure and act on the drivers to reverse adverse trends.

ABM is about management. This book is intended for 'general management' in any type of organization. The following chapters discuss the basic principles of the approach, describe how to approach the development of ABM models and the implementation of ABM thinking in a business, and use numerous case studies to illustrate how ABM can make a difference to business performance.

## KEY POINTS

- We know customers are important but without knowing the costs that customers impose on us, we'll never know which ones are profitable.

- When we know the costs that are driven by customer behaviours, we can differentiate the level of service we provide to various customer segments.

- In manufacturing businesses, direct labour, materials and components account for around two-thirds of total costs. The other, unmeasured, third is overhead activities and costs. In service industries, the unmeasured 'overhead' accounts for two-thirds or more of costs.

- ABM helps companies position themselves more advantageously in the market by providing accurate product and customer profitability information.

- ABM helps companies to improve their internal capability and lower unit costs.

- ABM is often seen as the preserve of the Finance function. In fact, its real strength lies in providing genuinely useful information for all functions in an organization.

- E-commerce channels currently give certain companies cost advantages. But not for long. Competitors will soon be doing the same thing.

- In e-commerce, customers want a share of lower costs, reflected in lower prices. In the future, it will be even more important to know customer profitability.

# Part I
# The Context

# 2 Historical perspective

## THE FIRST SERIOUS QUESTIONS

In the late 1980s and throughout the 1990s, the relevance of traditional accounting practices was seriously questioned. Conventional costing, budgeting and management accounts became ever less able to support the business decisions that were now relevant. The relevance debate was founded on three key criticisms.

The first criticism was levelled at the lack of technical developments in management accounting practice despite major changes in manufacturing technology. These major changes had resulted in greatly increased productivity, flexibility and quality, together with reduced lead times and inventory. Further, the significant changes in the proportions of 'direct' costs to 'overheads' had created major distortions in calculating product costs based on simplistic overhead recovery rates.

The second criticism held that management accounting was nothing more than financial reporting, leading to information that was too distorted, too aggregated and too late to be of much value to management.

The final criticism was concerned with the history of management accounting. A mature management accounting tradition was well established in the 1920s. In those days, traditional accounting had served business needs well in terms of cost management, management controls and performance measurement. However, the worldwide dominance of accountancy practice, standard training and examinations means that significant inertia towards change still exists.

The relevance discussions were published during a period of concerns over America's need to regenerate its industry in the context of the emergent global economy and the lessons from the success of Japan at that time. The moves in management accountancy were towards cost management and away from cost accounting. Developments since have included a concern with understanding such aspects as value-adding processes, life cycle costing, market-driven target costing, product and customer profitability, customer relationship management, Shareholder Value Added and the emergence of e-commerce.

# NEW COSTING APPROACHES GATHER PACE

Costs have been addressed in many ways in businesses, although traditional practice had formed around the major manufacturing sectors. The key problems with trying to determine accurate product costs started to gain the attention of a body called CAM-I (Consortium for Advanced Manufacturing – International). This body researches all aspects of the manufacturing sector in its struggle to come to terms with the changes that modern methods have introduced.

The CAM-I Cost Management Systems (CMS) Program is internationally recognized as a leading forum for the advancement of cost and resource management practices. Organized in 1986 as a coalition of leading thinkers from industry, government and academia, the CMS Program has accomplished extensive research and development of new management methods. The CMS Program is acknowledged worldwide for raising the awareness of Activity Based Costing (ABC) and Activity Based Management.

Although the manufacturing sector was the first to find that traditional accounting had lost its relevance, the service sector began to catch up. In financial services, what is a direct cost, and what is an overhead? Tracking the real cost of its products, services and customers became an issue as the recession and severe competition started to erode the traditional safe profits in banks and insurance companies.

In the utilities sector, the problem had grown rapidly with the changes in legislation that created greater competition. The 'regulator', who wanted to ensure visibility in a company's costs and put constant downward pressure on prices, further complicated the situation. Where there are virtual monopoly suppliers of services, the UK Monopolies and Mergers Commission is keen to gain access to the real costs of providing products and services, and handling customers.

Another perspective is through the value chain. The term Efficient Consumer Response (ECR) has been coined to encapsulate improving the chain that stretches from the basic raw material sources of a business through to the ultimate consumer. Generally, firms are only involved in part of the overall chain of value-creating activities, and therefore must endeavour to develop information that permits internal cost management and allows information to cross the company's boundaries. Activity-based approaches form the foundation on which information and costs are analysed throughout the value chain.

The new millennium has brought the prospect of a new dawn to many businesses. But all types of companies are finding that they are still in the dark. Their traditional accounting and costing methods remain unable to provide the answers to very relevant business questions, such as:

- How do we measure commercial success?
- Which parts of our process add value, or not?
- Do we make profitable products, and provide profitable services?
- Which is our most profitable customer?
- What can we afford to negotiate away?
- Which type of distributor is important to us?
- Do some products subsidize others, and if so, by how much?
- Are some of our customers targets for our competitors?
- Are we going for volume at the expense of profits?
- What is the real contribution from our product range?
- How should we invest this contribution from our current products?
- Should we go for new products or new markets?
- Will our new e-commerce channel provide the profits we yearn for?

Most of these questions have always been asked. It is management's job to answer them. But while struggling to feed ever more irrelevant budgeting systems and answer monthly management accounts variance queries, management has had to fall back on 'gut feel'. This is a poor substitute for appropriate information. ABM fills the chasm so long filled with inappropriate information.

## KEY POINTS

- The relevance of traditional accounting practices has been seriously questioned. Criticisms concern the distortions in calculating product costs based on simplistic overhead recovery rates, financial reporting that is too distorted to be of much value to management, and the worldwide dominance of accountancy practice, standard training and examinations, creating a significant inertia towards change.

- The foundations of ABM were built on the manufacturing sector, but the service sector has rapidly caught up, driven by regulatory and competitive pressures.

- Activity-based approaches form the foundation on which information and costs are analysed throughout the value chain.

- Traditional accounting and costing methods remain unable to provide the answers to very relevant business questions. ABM has filled the gap.

# 3   What is ABM?

Initially, Activity Based Costing (ABC) was presented as a means of establishing product costs more accurately. The emergence of Activity Based Management (ABM) provided a means of enhancing profitability. ABM is underpinned by a theory of resource consumption, with activities viewed as giving rise to costs, as in ABC, but taking the analysis further in a way that provides management with insights into managing the business overall. Essentially, these insights are focused on a process view of the business and a deeper understanding of product, channel and customer profitability.

## COSTING AND PROFITABILITY

The ledger, budgeting and monthly management accounts are based on reporting resources: those planned to be used, the consumption month on month and the variances from plan. Resources are those things that provide the means to allow work to be done in the organization: salary costs for the people doing the work, accommodation costs so that people can work in buildings, utilities so that people can see what they are doing and keep warm, vehicles so that goods can be delivered and customers visited. In some cases, the list of types of resource on the ledger may seem endless.

But no matter how long the list of resources, nothing in the ledger or the management accounts tells us how the resources are being consumed in doing things, to what purpose, or in what way. Resources are consumed by activities and it is at this level of analysis that we see what is actually being done. At this level we can also take a view on whether the *activities* that are being performed are necessary. We can also find out whether the activities are being done well and use the best methods, and so take the business forward, or whether they are really only sorting out problems that are dragging the business back.

13

Activities are undertaken for many purposes. Some directly manufacture products, while others indirectly support manufacture, such as the Quality department or materials handling. Some activities support the business as a whole, such as recruitment and training or the parts of the IT department that keep the network running.

Other activities are directly associated with customers, such as the salesforce, or more indirectly within the Credit Control department. Other parts of the business are working on activities to create a better future, such as New Product Development, and others are working on influencing potential customers, such as Marketing and Advertising.

Some parts of the business have little to do with products, services or customers but are necessary to keep the business legal, such as statutory reporting or organizing the shareholders' annual general meeting or preparing for the annual audit.

Activities are the very engine at the heart of the organization. Understanding what is done, how it is done, what causes it to be done and why we are doing it gives us a better chance of deciding whether we are getting the best value from the resources we deploy. As a simple analogy, budgeting and reporting on the different amount of food we eat may be mildly interesting but what people then do with their time having consumed the resources is what influences the world around them, for better or worse.

In conventional accounting, and particularly in manufacturing companies, costs are categorized into two main types: direct costs and overheads. Direct costs include the employees manufacturing the products, and the raw material they use. Overheads are the rest. The problem then arises when the costs of the products need to be calculated. Although we will look at this in greater detail in later chapters, we can say at this point that an ABM analysis accurately assigns the costs of those overheads that are actually influenced by the products being made or the services being provided.

Having derived accurate product costs, ABM goes further and analyses the costs of servicing each customer or specific segments of the customer base. Customers create a wide range of differing costs for a host of reasons.

The key insight that ABM exposes arises when revenue is brought into the equation. When the actual costs of the products or services going to a particular customer are calculated and the actual costs of servicing that customer derived, we can compare these figures to the revenue from the customer, as shown in Figure 3.1. Revenue minus the product costs gives the *ABM Product Contribution*. Revenue minus the product costs minus the costs of servicing the customer gives the *ABM Customer Contribution*. The sum of all the customer contributions has to pay for all those remaining costs that are not associated with the current products or customers, such as new product development and statutory accounting. Anything left after that is the profit.

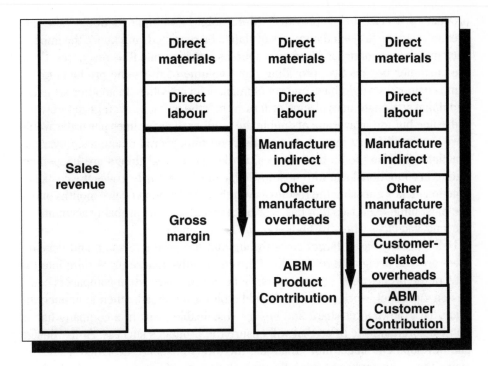

**Figure 3.1**   ABM Product and Customer Contributions

It is at the level of ABM Product or Customer Contribution that we use the term 'Product and Customer Profitability', as it is at this level that meaningful comparisons can be made between products and between customers. It is this type of analysis that exposes small or negative values prompting a serious review of which products or customers to keep, or at least a decision to take action to try to turn the relationship into one that provides positive contributions. We will look at this later in greater detail, as this insight into a company's costs is the central advantage of using ABM analysis.

By understanding how costs relate to those factors that drive the costs, we can use the powerful approach of Activity Based Budgeting (ABB). Rather than a futile circular argument revolving around resources, such as just asking for more people, the debate focuses on the drivers of cost that influence how much activity is actually required. ABB analyses the products or services to be produced, and so determines the level of the activities required. The level of activities then determines the resources to be budgeted. When automated, ABB can rapidly and accurately produce financial plans and models based on varying levels of volume assumptions.

The more obvious volume assumptions would take into account levels of product or service being provided. More subtle assumptions would take into account, say, the projected numbers of staff to be recruited, and hence the impacts back into the personnel and human resources activities, and thus resources. From the customer perspective, providing more volume of the same products to the same customers would have one set of impacts on activities. In another scenario, additional new customers placing orders for half the previous average quantity per order line but for an average of double the number of order lines per order would have a quite different impact on activities, and thus overall resources, in various functions. This is the stuff of the real world, where real things are happening. Sitting in a functional silo with no knowledge of what actually drives the costs in a function makes guessing the resources required for the next twelve months one of the most futile exercises that has ever been invented. This probably accounts for the long, sad faces when the budget round is announced.

Using activity-based target costs throughout the product design and development process brings the real world of the competitive marketplace right into the start of the process that creates costs. Gone are the days when companies could design a product, work out its costs, add a bit for overheads, then announce the price. To grab market share and ensure sustainable growth, a company has to know beforehand the price that will ensure the product's success. At the design and development stage, more than just the direct costs are designed in. At this stage, the company has to think through all aspects of the processes in the business affected by the product or service so that it does not breach the target cost.

## PROCESS IMPROVEMENT

An organization is a series of activities that combine in processes to create valuable products or services for customers. It is the effectiveness of an organization in performing these processes – to create high value at low cost – which marks out a successful company. Most of a company's significant processes travel across functional boundaries, and it is at these boundaries that delays and quality problems occur.

ABM focuses on the company's processes. If the processes are understood then failure activities can be eliminated from those processes. Value-adding activities can be examined to see whether better methods can be used. Time delays and quality issues can be addressed at the point in the process where they occur. ABM is the management of improvement through the analysis of business processes, and their associated activities. This analysis is carried out systematically and cross-functionally so that improvement projects can be readily implemented and the changes monitored.

ABM is an approach that involves many people within the organization, and is:

- a vehicle for creating process improvement – both incremental, continuous improvement and radical restructuring of the organization
- a model to show how costs (and revenues) are created through processes and activities – if you understand the activities, then you can understand the costs; if you understand the processes, then you understand the business
- a means of measuring the company's progress in the key areas of the business that need change and improvement.

We will look at this use of ABM in greater detail later, as the insights gained from process analysis are central to reducing unit costs, eliminating waste and improving levels of service to customers.

Although ABM can be used to address a specific project or process that needs improvement, it is at its most effective when the company uses ABM as a standard approach to business improvement. This way, the entire organization can be involved in process improvement, and over time every process within the company can be studied, and changes initiated.

## KEY POINTS

- Nothing in the ledger or the management accounts tells us how resources are being consumed in doing things, to what purpose, or in what way.

- Activity analysis allows us to find out whether the activities are being done well and use the best methods to take the business forward, or whether they are really only sorting out problems that are dragging the business back.

- Revenue minus the total product costs gives the *ABM Product Contribution*. Revenue minus the product costs minus the total costs of servicing the customer gives the *ABM Customer Contribution*.

- The sum of all the customer contributions has to pay for all those remaining costs that are not associated with the current products or customers, such as new product development and statutory accounting. Anything left after that is the profit.

- It is at the level of ABM Product or Customer Contribution that we use the term 'Product and Customer Profitability', as it is at this level that meaningful comparisons can be made between products and between customers.

- Activity Based Budgeting (ABB) focuses on the drivers of cost that influence how much activity is actually required. ABB analyses the products or services to be produced, and so determines the level of the activities required. The level of activities then determines the resources to be budgeted.

17

- An organization is a series of activities that combine in processes to create valuable products or services for customers. It is the effectiveness of an organization in performing these processes which marks out a successful company.

- ABM includes the management of improvement through the analysis of business processes, and their associated activities.

# 4 Frameworks for measurement and improvement

Although ABM can be used as a stand-alone approach to understand processes, product and customer costs and profitability, it provides a more powerful means of decision support if it exists as part of a larger framework of measures.

Over the years, a number of frameworks have been developed, each endeavouring to arrive at a more rounded perspective on the business and a reduced emphasis on the previous domination of financial measures.

Although traditionally profit has assumed the dominant role as a measure, the many means of its attainment are recognized as being much more varied and complex to measure and control. Consequently, as well as being concerned with sales and margins, it is necessary to have information on such things as production times, component commonality, quality initiatives, customer satisfaction, customer service activity, employee skill development, employee turnover, legislation changes, environmental impacts and many other variables in the business. In fact, any element of performance can be important if it is related to success in the marketplace. Their integration has been more formally recognized by the use of a number of frameworks that attempt to bring a more rational balance to the variety of measures used in the business. ABM is a key component of these measurement frameworks.

## THE BALANCED SCORECARD

Professors Kaplan and Norton first described the *Balanced Scorecard* in an article in the *Harvard Business Review* in 1992. The term 'balanced' reflects the objective of reporting to stakeholders other than the owners of the business, as well as in ways quite different to financial reporting. The Balanced Scorecard includes four perspectives, as shown in Figure 4.1. As well as the more traditional measures found in the financial perspective, the scorecard includes customer, internal business, and learning perspectives.

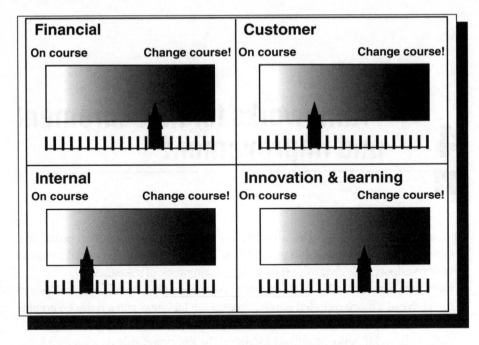

**Figure 4.1**   The four perspectives of the Balanced Scorecard

The customer perspective can include measures of quality, lead times, reliability and customer service as these impact on customer satisfaction, repeat business and referrals. The internal business perspective is concerned with processes and productivity. Crucially, there is a recognition that the workforce is a vital stakeholder whose skills and commitment to the organization cannot be taken for granted. The fourth perspective, that of learning and innovation, is concerned with performance improvements and the ability to introduce successful new products and services. All four perspectives reflect the need to sustain a strategic position in the marketplace to create value for shareholders, provide challenging employment opportunities for the workforce and enjoy a sustained partnership with customers, both corporate and consumers. It is therefore imperative that an appropriate range of measures exists to integrate in the scorecard.

A by-product of using a Balanced Scorecard is that, throughout the organization, it raises the awareness of measures, in a language that people can understand in their own areas of responsibility and influence. However, where useful information is lacking, ABM becomes a powerful tool to understand and answer fundamental questions that arise around processes, products and customers. Profitable customers served by ineffective processes will not lead to success. Impeccable processes serving unprofitable customer segments will also drag the company down. If employees focus their learning and innovation on products and services that attract disproportionately high but largely invisible costs, it can bring a business to its knees. The Balanced Scorecard by itself is not a guarantee of corporate success. The underlying behaviour of costs and an understanding of what drives costs provide the knowledge and insights to drive improvements. In this respect, ABM is a fundamental building block.

## THE BUSINESS EXCELLENCE MODEL

The European Foundation for Quality Management (EFQM) Business Excellence Model arose during the time that 'quality' and 'total quality' had ascended to the highest point of management's consciousness. The quality movement had tended to follow the course of ISO 9000, an international standard that focuses on quality systems within the business. In response to this trend, a number of companies leading the quality movement searched for a means of describing a business across a range of features that went beyond just looking at the internal quality systems.

This endeavour led to the formation of the EFQM and the publication of the Business Excellence Model. The model defines nine elements as shown in Figure 4.2. Five elements are known as *enablers*, and the remaining four are the *results*. Each element has a weighting, and when taken as a score, a company with a total of 80 per cent or more is recognized as achieving excellence. In Europe, such high scores put a company in the running for the annual European Quality Awards.

Interestingly, a company that states that it has implemented ABM as an approach to inform and change its scoring on a number of elements only achieves an enhanced score if it actually produces the ABM information and acts on it.

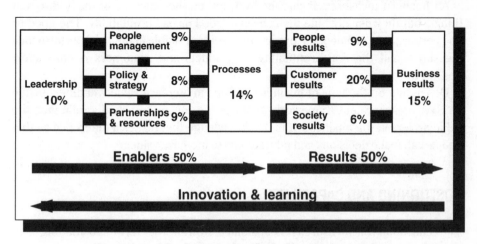

**Figure 4.2** The nine elements of the Business Excellence Model

Setting up an ABM programme but failing to apply its findings will count against a company.

## SHAREHOLDER VALUE ADDED

The measure of Shareholder Value Added (SVA) is unashamedly financial. SVA, the generic term (also known as Economic Value Added), was introduced as a measure by the American consulting firm Stern Stewart & Co. Their term and the three-letter acronym, EVA are both trademarks of their company. The definition is simply: Shareholder Value Added equals the net operating profit after tax minus the capital charge.

The net operating profit after tax brings into focus prices, volumes, the cost of sales and all the operating expenses in the business, as well as taxes. It is therefore imperative that the business knows which products and customers are profitable, and why, and that its processes operate at the lowest unit cost. Whatever techniques or approaches are used to achieve these ends, it is important that information in the business is structured to support the right decision-making. ABM is a building block to create this knowledge.

The *capital charge* is all capital (net working capital plus net fixed capital) multiplied by the cost of capital. Capital comprises working capital (debtors, creditors and inventory) plus fixed capital (property, plant and equipment). Actions to reduce debtor days and work in progress would be simple examples of increasing the value in the business. Investing in capital equipment focused on profitable products to profitable customers requires greater finesse in ensuring that the right decisions are made.

All financial measures, including SVA, tell us the outcome of many different things, but they usually hide the causes of good or bad profitability. The good or bad performance of individual processes is seldom visible in financial performance measures, and the real profitability of products and customers is completely obscured.

Depending on the type of business, actions to increase value will differ. Inside an SVA measurement framework, ABM is the means to actually influence the value drivers in the business. It is this knowledge that makes a difference so that people can make decisions and take actions to increase value.

## POSITIONING AND CAPABILITY

The collection of measures encapsulated within the term 'positioning and capability' was developed by the UK consulting firm Develin & Partners, and is

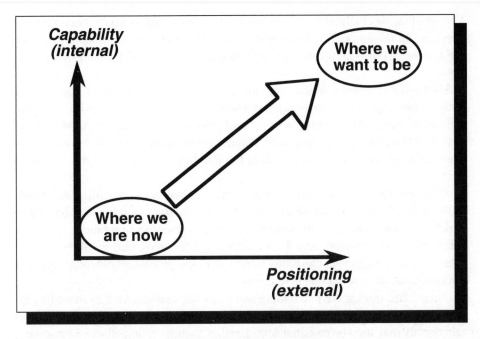

**Figure 4.3    The journey of change**

founded on the principle that organizations need to make a series of steps from where they are now to some future goal. To guide the company on its journey to a future goal, a 'map' is required, where the axes of the map are *positioning* and *capability*. The basic map is shown in Figure 4.3.

Positioning is to do with external factors, such as:

- understanding customer needs
- understanding product and customer profitability
- understanding competitor initiatives
- determining the business's financial needs
- complying with changing legislation
- meeting environmental constraints.

Getting positioning right leads to higher levels of revenue through providing profitable products and services, increasing market share, increasing the size of the market, and by retaining profitable customers.

Capability is to do with internal factors, such as:

- key business processes
- procedures and systems
- competencies, skills, education and training
- attitudes, style and behaviours.

23

The capability is changed to deliver the desired positioning. Capability creates the costs in the business. The journey joins revenue and cost. Getting the balance right between positioning and capability enhances profits and the value of the business.

ABM is the vehicle by which companies journey along their chosen route. ABM informs key aspects of positioning, particularly when used to provide accurate product costing and to derive product and customer profitability. ABM informs key aspects of capability, particularly when used to understand process costs, failures within processes, and to establish the link between costs and the drivers of cost.

ABM provides the basis for management to make better informed decisions, both on positioning and capability. In other words, the company can determine which products, markets and customer segments it wishes to retain, it can make relative pricing decisions based on competitor initiatives, and it will be able to focus on those aspects of capability which leverage profitability through process improvement and a reduction in unit costs.

Using ABM during the positioning work provides an opportunity to undertake customer engineering as an action to guide changes in capability. Avoiding a certain activity may then be an initial action, rather than spending effort on improving what could be an unnecessary process. ABM analysis of the current business, prior to making changes to any processes, can answer a number of positioning questions:

- Can the salesforce be directed towards more profitable segments in relation to the costs of servicing the business that is generated?
- Will a switch away from volume selling to focused selling improve short-term profitability?
- Can some customers or product lines be dropped and achieve an increase in company profitability?
- Can we apply discounts more effectively to achieve volume and know that we will remain profitable?
- Can we switch some customers to wholesalers or other third parties, rather than service every customer ourselves?

ABM is the way to link a company's trading relationships (positioning) to its internal cost structure (capability). The basic premise is that activities consume resources and convert them into products and services to customers. Costs are therefore the consequence of resource decisions, and income is the consequence of linked activities, the business processes. The requirement is therefore to improve resourcing decisions as the means of managing costs, and to improve processes as the means of improving business effectiveness and thus customer service and revenue.

In the positioning and capability framework, ABM plays a key role in informing the journey. On the positioning axis, ABM is used for profitability management, such as costing and profitability analysis, customer and product mix decisions, and support for marketing decisions. On the capability axis, ABM is used for resource and performance management, such as resource and service level changes, activity-based budgeting and cost driver analysis, and for process improvement to eliminate process failures and reduce unit costs.

## KEY POINTS

- The integration of many elements of performance has been more formally recognized by the use of a number of frameworks that attempt to bring a more rational balance to the variety of measures used in the business. ABM is a key component of these measurement frameworks.

- The *Balanced Scorecard* includes four perspectives: financial, customer, internal business, and learning. The underlying behaviour of costs and an understanding of what drives costs provide the knowledge and insights to drive improvements. In this respect, ABM is a fundamental building block.

- The EFQM's Business Excellence Model defines nine elements. Five elements are known as *enablers* and the remaining four are the *results*. ABM is an approach to inform and improve the scoring on a number of elements.

- Shareholder Value Added equals the net operating profit after tax minus the capital charge. ABM is the means to influence the value drivers in the business that will help increase SVA.

- Positioning is to do with external factors, and getting this right leads to higher levels of revenue through providing profitable products and services, increasing market share, increasing the size of the market, and by retaining profitable customers.

- Capability is to do with internal factors, a change to which delivers the desired positioning. Capability creates the costs in the business. Positioning and capability thus join revenue and cost. Getting the balance right enhances profits and the value of the business.

- The journey of change can be mapped using the two axes of *positioning* and *capability*. ABM provides the information for both axes, to plan the journey and measure how far you have travelled.

# 5   The ABM framework

In Chapter 4, we saw how ABM fits into a number of overarching frameworks of measurement and improvement. In Chapter 6, we will see how ABM is used in a real-life example, to illustrate how ABM handles costs, assigning them to activities then onwards to products, channels and customers.

However, before going into an example it is wise to take a few moments to describe how ABM views the treatment of costs, which differentiates it from traditional accounting approaches. This chapter explains the way ABM handles costs and the characteristics of activities compared to conventional approaches, as well as introducing the language of ABM.

## TRADITIONAL RESOURCE ACCOUNTING

Most established accounting systems usually capture and distribute resource costs based on one or more of the following methods:

1. organization structure or cost centre accounting
2. budgetary accounting
3. cost allocation accounting.

From their longevity of practice, we must assume that in the past they have met the needs of organizations to some degree. Yet every one of them fails to meet the full requirement for management information that will adequately support decision-making in today's competitive environment.

### COST CENTRE ACCOUNTING

This is a popular method for applying resource costs to an organization. The accounting system identifies each of the organizational parts of the traditional functional structure and applies the identifiable costs to that part of the structure.

In many traditional organizations, the only costs that are identified to the organization's functional departments are the salary costs. Although overhead costs are sometimes distributed to cost centres, it is more common to find that these costs are ignored at the unit level. Many overhead costs are held centrally by the providers of services, and not sub-divided to the users of the services. For example, the cost of 'vehicles' would be held in the function or department that looks after the vehicles. The cost of 'postage' would be held in the postroom where the mailing physically takes place.

This system was created to provide management with some information on the costs of the organization's departments. Some argued at the time that this would make 'controllable' costs visible to those managers that have to control the costs. However, under cost pressure the owners of resources supplied to others would turn the tap down or off. The Stationery department refusing to issue paper for other departments' photocopiers is a result of this approach to cost control.

Where attempts to obtain a true picture of departmental costs are applied, managers of resources that are supplied to others apply cross-charges to users, based on a rate for the service. The rate is based on a collection of costs the service department actually incurs, such as its own staff salaries, to which it adds a mysterious amount to cover its own overheads and the costs that it has received as cross-charges from others. The cross-charging game can reach heights of absurdity when internal sub-divisions of the organization are made into profit centres. The charge-out rate then includes a bit extra, which it calls 'profit'. In some instances, this accumulating figure is then used to purchase something from outside on the basis that it is using spare income, and not a departmental cost. From the organization's perspective, this is real money going out the door. However, trying to get accurate costs to the place in the organization where the budget for the funds is held can also create absurd situations, as the following example aptly illustrates.

## CASE STUDY

A company introduced a simple method to improve the cost-effectiveness of the use of taxis. By arranging to use a single supplier, any travellers only had to print and sign their name against the meter cost recorded on the taxi's log sheet. To prevent fraud, the passenger retained a tear-off copy slip showing the cost. On a monthly basis, the taxi company presented its itemized bill, which a clerk in Accounts dutifully used to look up where each passenger worked. The cost centre manager's name and cost centre number were also looked up and noted. The annotated invoice then started its journey around the site for each manager to authorize and add the cost centre allocation number for taxi journeys to the invoice. Later, these costs would be accumulated and reported to each cost centre manager.

Three months later, the irate taxi company would begin to demand payment. The problem for the Accounts department was knowing where the invoice was in its journey around the site. In a year, 40 per cent of the invoices never found their way back to the Finance function. The taxi company would regularly threaten court action to secure payment. Accounts Payable would just ask for a faxed copy of the invoice and pay the same day on receipt of the fax.

Finally, someone did question whether the whole process added any value, or whether it just added unnecessary cost.

In all this striving for accuracy, accountability and control, hardly any real attempt is ever made to trace costs to the activities or process flows in organizations or to the ultimate output, the products and services for customers.

## BUDGETARY ACCOUNTING

The tracking of costs to a budgetary account is often combined with cost centre accounting. In this case, the major concern of the spenders of resources is to ensure that their total expenditures do not exceed the allocated budgetary amounts. Consequently, accounting systems become a safeguard mechanism to capture commitments, undelivered orders, and expenditures, normally divided into the cost centres that reflect the organization structures, to enable tracking of actuals, budgets and variances. The measure of success, and thus the major objective of each accountable manager, is to use the resources assigned fully, rather than enhancing productivity or reducing expenses. In some types of organization, any attempt to conserve resources or work more effectively to come under budget runs the risk of prompting a reduction in the future budget resource level. The budgetary control mechanism can reach heights of absurdity.

### CASE STUDY

In a government research organization, the scientists received funds to undertake research projects. Towards the financial year end, the researchers had unspent funds, but there were insufficient hours of research capacity to conduct the research before the year end. The fund providers wanted the funds spent (for fear of their own funds for the following year being reduced), but were only concerned that the money was spent on 'project-related' costs. In this case, buying equipment was acceptable. As specialist equipment would be pointless, the researchers looked for something more generic. Two weeks later, three large vehicles arrived on site delivering top-of-the-range-desktop computers.

As there was no immediate scientific purpose for the computers, they remained in their boxes and researchers used them as additional seats. Among the support departments, frustrations reached boiling point when they saw the vehicles being unloaded. The cap on their costs always prevented them procuring decent equipment. Worse was to come. Given the different funding regimes for the two groups, the overhead functions were not allowed to use the spare computers languishing in their boxes.

Like cost centre accounting systems, budgetary control mechanisms make no attempt to cost the outputs of all the work, or in many cases to even bother to define the output. If real customers are at the end of a supply chain of activities in such environments, then their needs can be well down the list of priorities, with 'meeting the budget' firmly at the top.

## COST ALLOCATION ACCOUNTING

Where an organization has the characteristics of a business then it generally has a need to distribute its costs to an output so that it can price its products or services. Revenues also come into the picture, and we talk about 'revenues minus total cost leaves us the profit'. To make the costs visible, 'true' cost accounting systems were established to capture and distribute costs to the outputs, such as goods or services. These cost accounting systems use the classic model of cost distribution which was designed around the major sector of the economy at the time: manufacturing. In this system, the focus of gathering costs and collecting them under generic headings relied upon the simple classifications of direct labour, direct materials, and overhead. Businesses and business-like organizations have relied upon the historical model of cost accounting for over a hundred years.

However, the traditional cost accounting methodology does create significant inaccuracies in output costs because of the manner in which overhead costs are apportioned to output rather than assigned or traced to output. When this erroneous method of cost distribution finds its way into the ultimate price of the output, it leads to poor management decisions about which products or services to promote hard, or which to discontinue, and which customers it should sell to or drop.

As traditional accounting has such a grip on most organizations, we would argue that it is in the areas of the fundamental flaws it contains that ABM really makes a difference. In particular, ABM is superior to traditional accounting in a number of ways:

- ABM provides visibility in the way costs flow through the business.
- ABM establishes the links between activities and those factors, internal or external, that drive the level of activity up or down.
- ABM eliminates the false divide between direct costs and overheads.
- ABM separates out those costs that deal with today's business from those that secure the future.
- ABM ignores gross margin and uses accurate product and customer contributions as the basis for comparing product and customer profitability.
- ABM exchanges functional myopia for a cross-functional process view of the organization.
- ABM exchanges the stilted definitions of value-added and non-value-added for sensitive categories that highlight the subtle impact of internal process failures and external customer behaviour.

## ABM VERSUS TRADITIONAL TREATMENTS OF COSTS

At many levels, ABM brings a different perspective to how costs are treated. ABM challenges the traditional approaches to product costing, gross margins, profitability, functions and hierarchies, value-added and non-value-added, and budgeting.

### TRADITIONAL PRODUCT COSTING

It is in the area of product costing that serious weaknesses in the traditional approach first became a cause for concern. In the days when traditional accounting practices were being formed and internationalized, the dominant industries were in the manufacturing sector. In a typical large manufacturing company, there would be large numbers of employees concerned with direct manufacturing and a much smaller number in the overhead departments.

In a situation where the direct labour costs could be as high as 90 per cent and overheads 10 per cent of total costs, it was important to achieve some accuracy in terms of the hours, and therefore costs, required to make components and assemblies. Work-study and other techniques found a ready use in determining the direct labour content of any product. The direct material costs were also simple to calculate for each product, based on raw material content, scrap rates, bought-out parts and so on. Working out how much of the overhead activity was actually associated with each product was seen as a lot of effort for such a small improvement in the accuracy of the product cost. This led to the use of the Overhead Recovery Rate (ORR) as the fundamental method of product costing.

To derive a method of calculating the proportion of overheads to allocate to each product, a simple ratio was derived, known as the ORR. A company would simply find the overall ratio between total overhead costs and total direct labour, say 10 per cent. The direct labour for each product made, and any new ones developed, would then have 10 per cent added to account for the overhead, and so give the product cost.

As manufacturing became more complex, the proportion of overhead activities to direct activities started to increase. Product costs now became far more sensitive to the indirect and overhead costs associated with each product. The traditional ORR became highly suspect as a means of calculating product costs. Some products could be seriously under-costed, and thus probably highly competitive, but an increase in sales volume would actually erode profitability. Conversely, over-costed products would be unattractively priced, and few sales made.

As the proportion of overhead costs increased in a business, the more serious the distortion in product costing became through using the ORR method.

## ABM PRODUCT COSTING

In ABM, the indirect and overhead costs are determined for each product. The characteristics of two products can be quite different in the way they need overhead activity to support manufacture.

### CASE STUDY

A company that had traditionally made its name manufacturing bogies for railway trucks and carriages had branched out into making braking systems for long-haul diesel road vehicles. While the technology surrounding the railway business had not developed significantly over the years, the road vehicle technologies had advanced in complexity at a rapid rate. Using direct labour as the determinant of the proportion of overhead costs had led to over-priced railway products and under-priced road vehicle products. The growth in the road vehicle business then seriously eroded overall profits, and the stable rail business was drifting to competitors.

Figure 5.1 shows two of the company's products costed using the conventional ORR, in this case 300 per cent. For product Pr1, the direct labour had 50 units of cost, so the manufacturing overhead was assumed to be 300 per cent of this: 150 units of cost. Product Pr2 again used 300 per cent, and this was applied to the direct labour cost of 200 units, giving a manufacturing overhead of 600 units of cost. Using a conventional ORR took no account of the real differences in the amount of overheads that either product required.

**Conventional approach**

| | Products | |
| --- | --- | --- |
| | Pr1 | Pr2 |
| Direct material | 200 | 100 |
| Direct labour | 50 | 200 |
| *Calculate overhead using ORR based on direct labour* | *50 x 300%* | *200 x 300%* |
| Calculated production overhead | 150 | 600 |
| Total direct + overhead | 400 | 900 |
| Revenue | 1250 | 1300 |
| Gross margin | 1000 | 1000 |
| Product contribution | 850 | 400 |

**Figure 5.1**  Conventional product costing

Product Pr1, a road vehicle braking system, was complex, had many production changes, and used difficult manufacturing technology. There were also many discussions with specialist suppliers.

Product Pr2, a railway truck bogie, used simple manufacturing technology, enjoyed a steady demand with few changes to schedules, and had used the same suppliers of raw material over a long period.

Using the ABM approach, the direct and actual overhead costs reflected the real situation, as shown in Figure 5.2. Note that for Pr1 the conventional approach gave a contribution nearly double what it actually was. In other words, in reality the product was less profitable than they thought. Conversely, Pr2 was much more profitable than they thought. Using the overhead recovery approach meant that Pr1 was under-priced. They had orders, but made little profit. Sales of Pr2 could be higher if it wasn't over-priced.

| Conventional approach | | | ABM approach | | |
|---|---|---|---|---|---|
| | Products | | | Products | |
| | Pr1 | Pr2 | | Pr1 | Pr2 |
| Direct material | 200 | 100 | Direct material | 200 | 100 |
| Direct labour | 50 | 200 | Direct labour | 50 | 200 |
| *Calculate overhead using ORR based on direct labour* | *50 x 300%* | *200 x 300%* | Actual overhead activity costs | | |
| | | | *Purchasing* | *120* | *30* |
| | | | *Planning* | *50* | *80* |
| | | | *Material handling* | *100* | *50* |
| | | | *Inspection* | *180* | *40* |
| | | | *Maintenance* | *80* | *20* |
| Calculated production overhead | 150 | 600 | ABM production overhead | 530 | 220 |
| Total direct + overhead | 400 | 900 | Total direct + overhead | 780 | 520 |
| Revenue | 1250 | 1300 | Revenue | 1250 | 1300 |
| Gross margin | 1000 | 1000 | Gross margin | 1000 | 1000 |
| Product contribution | 850 | 400 | Product contribution | 470 | 780 |

**Figure 5.2**   Comparing product costing methods

## TRADITIONAL VIEW OF GROSS MARGIN

In traditional accounting, we find the term 'gross margin', defined as the revenue minus the direct costs. As long as the gross margin is a positive number, then the product is deemed to make a 'contribution to overheads'. In other words, whatever the overheads actually are, at least there are some funds to pay for them. The issue is that we do not know, other than at the overall company level, whether this contribution has any bearing whatsoever on the real overheads involved in producing each particular product.

## ABM VIEW OF PRODUCT CONTRIBUTION (PRODUCT PROFITABILITY)

In the product costing examples above, the ABM analysis uncovered the actual indirect and overhead costs associated with producing each product. Now when we calculate the revenue less the actual product costs, we have a number that is called the ABM Product Contribution. In other words, if this is a positive number, then we know that product costs are covered and the sum left over now contributes to the other overhead costs in the business such as sales, R&D, invoicing and so on.

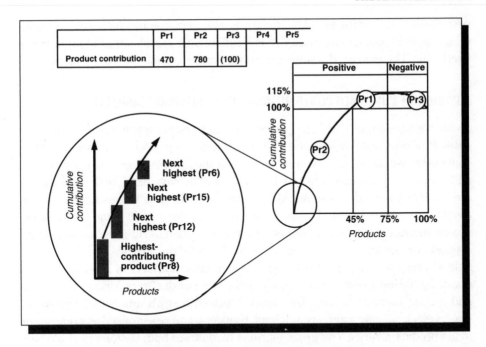

| | Pr1 | Pr2 | Pr3 | Pr4 | Pr5 |
|---|---|---|---|---|---|
| Product contribution | 470 | 780 | (100) | | |

**Figure 5.3**   The cumulative product contribution curve

The ABM Product Contribution is a fairer basis on which to compare one product with another. We can show each product on a graph where we plot the cumulative product contribution, highest to lowest, for all the products. The resulting graph, the appropriately named 'hook curve' is shown in Figure 5.3. The hook curve is one of the most powerful ways to display the outcome of the ABM analysis.

As we would expect, one product is something of a cash cow, such as Pr1, The traditional gross margin calculation also gave a high figure, and we now know that there are no issues concerning high levels of indirect and overhead activity. However, as we add more and more products to the graph, such as Pr2, we eventually find those where the revenue only just covers the real costs of manufacturing. The ABM Product Contribution gets smaller and smaller until some products balance out to zero.

At the tail end, we might be unfortunate to discover that some products, such as Pr3, have a negative ABM Product Contribution. In other words, the revenue we obtain is insufficient to cover the actual manufacturing costs of the direct materials and labour and the appropriately assigned indirect and overhead costs. What is often surprising is finding products in this category where the gross margin is positive. We believe that the situation is acceptable as long as they are making 'a contribution' to overheads. The reality is that any volume increase seriously erodes overall profitability, rather than building up a useful contribution to cover overheads. The increased volume contributes only to losing even more money.

## ABM VIEW OF CUSTOMER CONTRIBUTION (CUSTOMER PROFITABILITY)

So far, we have emphasized comparing revenue to actual product costs to give the ABM Product Contribution. This contribution has to pay for a number of significant costs associated with winning the sales in the first place, getting the products and services to the customers and, finally, collecting payments. All these activities are customer-related costs. An ABM analysis of these activities enables us to assign the customer-related costs to each of the customers. In some cases, focusing on individual customers will be appropriate whereas, in others, meaningful segments or groups of customers will be the basis for the analysis.

In a particular company, Customer X placed large numbers of low-value orders manually, raised many queries, made many returns due to ordering errors, and had a poor payment history. Customer Y placed a small number of high-value orders electronically, paid through bank transfers, and never raised any queries or made product returns. The gross margins made from both customers could well be equal, but the costs of doing business with one are significantly higher. By calculating revenue minus the real costs of the products the customer is ordering and minus the real cost of servicing the customer, we are left with the ABM Customer Contribution. This figure is an appropriate basis on which to compare one customer to another.

We can now plot a graph of cumulative customer contribution, highest to lowest, for each customer. Again, we would generally find a hook curve, but usually flatter than for the products. Many customers could be giving no contribution at all, as shown in Figure 5.4, with some seriously eroding profitability.

Again, as we would expect, one customer could well be a cash cow. The traditional gross margin calculation gave a high figure, and we now know that there are no issues concerning high levels of overhead activity associated with the customer. However, as we add more and more customers to the graph, we find some where the revenue only just covers the real costs of the products and the real costs of servicing the customer. The ABM Customer Contribution gets smaller and smaller until some customers balance out to zero.

At the tail end, we might be unfortunate to discover that some customers have a negative ABM Customer Contribution: in other words, the revenue we obtain is insufficient to cover the actual manufacturing costs plus the customer servicing costs. What is often surprising is that customers in this category may have positive gross margins. Again, we believe that the situation is acceptable as long as they are making 'a contribution' to overheads. The reality is that any volume increase

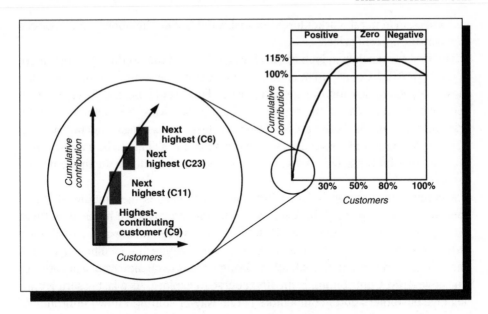

**Figure 5.4** The cumulative customer contribution curve

seriously erodes overall profitability, rather than building up a useful contribution to cover overheads.

At the start of Chapter 1, we said that we know, instinctively, that some customers are more profitable than others. We also know that some are probably loss-making. We may also have some idea of which customers are probably the least profitable and which are the most profitable. So anecdotal evidence will pick up the extremes. The hook curve shows the situation with the other 99 per cent. This is often a profound shock to management. With accurate information we are now in a position to explore how we can change the relationship with the customer, and thus the costs incurred. In extreme cases, we might consider ceasing to do business with the customer.

The appropriately named hook curves are a revelation to many companies that undertake an ABM analysis. Previously hidden from view by the smokescreen of gross margins, the realities of products that lose money and customers that lose money are now shown in sharp relief. The question then arises: what to do about the low or negative ABM Contributions? The immediate reaction is likely to be an instant desire to get rid of the products and customers which are in the negative part of the hook curve. However, caution should be the first response. It is in this area that the hidden additional profit lurks. The approach should be to convert the negatives into additional positives. The quick answer is to raise prices for the products or specific customers. While this may seem fair, particularly to 'awkward' customers, in general market forces probably determine the upper limit on prices – usually the current prices!

The first approach is to look at the characteristics of the products or customers in the high ABM Contribution end of the hook curve, and then attempt to create these characteristics for the negative area. This would be the 'best practice' approach. In some cases, the processes that interact with the customer may be creating problems for both parties. Resolving these types of issue opens up a constructive dialogue with customers where the outcome is likely to be a reduction in process costs for both. This is a win–win solution, and should be the first outcome to search for.

Another consideration before eliminating customers is the amount of 'fixed' costs that may be affected. In ABM, we argue that no costs are fixed; all of them can be influenced in some way. However, for a warehousing and distribution business, it is not easy to reduce the size of the warehousing facilities or vehicle fleet in the short term. In this situation, taking actions to change from a negative to a positive ABM Contribution is the first course to explore. As a last resort, letting negative customers go to competitors is one way of shifting known unprofitable business to other companies that will be glad of the volume but will not be aware of the unprofitable nature of the business. The impact of volume and ABM Contribution can be shown graphically in a way that helps to determine the next course of action to take. Figure 5.5 shows a number of customers on a graph of the percentage ABM Customer Contribution divided by sales revenue set against total

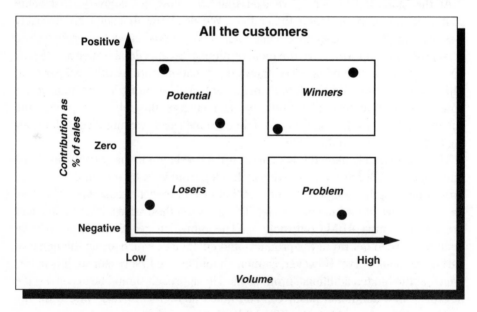

**Figure 5.5** Customer contribution and volume

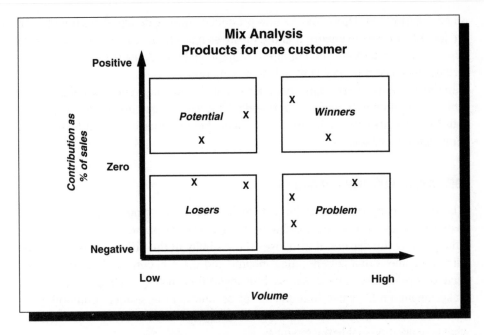

**Figure 5.6** Product contribution and volume

sales revenue per customer. This highlights which customers are priorities to tackle.

For any one customer, a graph can be plotted of the percentage ABM Product Contribution set against total sales value for each product the customer buys, as shown in Figure 5.6. This highlights which products are priorities to resolve for that customer. What if a particular customer is ordering a mix of products, where one or more products has a negative ABM Product Contribution? It does not automatically follow that you should tell the customer that they cannot have a particular product any more. This issue demands taking a balanced view about the future relationship. It may pay overall to leave the situation as it is if the overall relationship is sufficiently profitable.

The key to using an ABM analysis is that a business makes decisions with knowledge that it can trust.

## TRADITIONAL VIEW OF COSTS IN A BUSINESS

As we have said earlier, in traditional accounting a business reports the use of resources, and may split these simply into direct costs and overheads. However, in the overhead departments there exists a large diversity of costs. There may be training and personnel departments that enhance the skills and competencies of other departments. There may be new product or service design departments that are looking at ways to ensure that the business has a future. There may be a legal department that looks at such things as litigation taken against the business or the formulation of commercial contracts to new markets.

In the accounts, these costs are expensed under headings such as 'Salaries' and lumped together as business overheads. This simple categorization of diverse activities obscures the rich diversity of tasks being undertaken in a business to serve many purposes.

## ABM VIEW OF COSTS IN A BUSINESS

Where a company allocates all its costs to products and customers (full absorption costing) it loses the real relationship between cost drivers and those costs that are influenced by the drivers. It also loses the visibility of the difference between the current business that is generating income and the real contribution that can be used to develop the future business. Full absorption costing destroys the ability to make meaningful relative judgements of product and customer profitability. In ABM, the diverse costs and activities are categorized so that we can understand what is happening inside the business.

There are certain key activities that are being performed that we define as *front-line*. A frontline activity is one that has something to do with producing the primary product or service and any activities that interface with customers. Frontline activities have a direct cause-and-effect relationship to products and customers through cost drivers. This relationship may be a simple one based on, say, production hours to produce a product or number of invoices processed for each customer. They are current costs paid for by the revenue from current products and services for current customers. If more volume of the cost driver is forecast, then more resources will be required. However, changing the methods used can change the unit cost of doing the work.

There are other costs and activities that exist because the organization is a legal entity and must fulfil specific requirements. The annual audit and financial reporting would fall into this category. Such costs are largely independent of the product or service being provided. They are the costs of being in business. These we call *infrastructure*. These costs and activities have no direct relationship to current or future products and services. The level of costs is unlikely to change with variations in throughput volumes or number of customers. However, the actual costs can change if the method changes or a service is obtained at a lower rate. For example, the auditors can be changed in order to reduce the level of fees charged.

In most organizations, doing nothing to develop future products and services will guarantee the demise of the business. Organizations need to have funds to pay for the current costs of the people undertaking, say, new product development, but the benefits are expected to be derived in the future. The current product through-puts or current customers do not directly influence these activities. We call these activities *sustaining* and they are essentially an investment to achieve a return in the future. The organization has a choice over the level of sustaining costs it wants to have. A reduction in sustaining costs would transfer directly to the bottom line, but it would risk the future of the business. Companies invest in sustaining costs so that they will make a higher return in the future. It could be argued that sustaining costs should be made specifically visible to shareholders, as they are investments in the business made out of retained profits that could have been distributed.

The final category we call *internal service*. Typically, training, recruitment, current use of IT networks and the like are an internal service to all the other departments in the organization. There are no direct relationships to current products and customers other than through the frontline activities that are supported. The key here is to understand and then assign the internal service costs and activities in an appropriate manner to all the other areas of the business that are supported.

Given the four categories of costs and activities, we can now structure the costs in an ABM model in a way that is far more meaningful than using conventional accounting categories, and thus improve decision-making.

Having analysed the activities in an organization, the first task is to reassign the internal service costs and activities to those of frontline, sustaining and infrastructure. This uplifts the frontline costs and links the cost drivers to the internal service costs. One can imagine a need for more frontline staff in, say, the Invoicing department, requiring an increase in the Training department to train more invoice clerks. The link may be the number of people trained per annum, which would be the cost driver volume. The uplifted frontline activities are assigned to the products and customers. The ABM Contributions are the revenue minus the uplifted frontline costs, either at customer or product level. It is at this point that it is meaningful to compare ABM Contributions for each product and for each customer. This is what product and customer profitability means in ABM. The total ABM Customer Contribution has to pay for the infrastructure costs. After that, any amount that is left has to pay for any sustaining costs and activities the company has determined it needs to secure its future. Increasing sustaining costs reduces profit to shareholders. This is the acid test of management's decision to spend on sustaining activities.

The four ABM categories of cost are not shown in the accounts. However, these categories identify more clearly the nature of the decisions that management is called upon to make. They also focus management on two clear objectives:

1. to ensure that cost-effective methods are used to produce current products to current customers at a price that generates the maximum positive ABM Product and Customer Contributions
2. to ensure that the ABM Contributions are used effectively to generate new products and services to new markets such that the return on the investment in sustaining costs is greater than that which would be achieved by shareholders investing elsewhere.

## TRADITIONAL VIEW OF FUNCTIONS AND HIERARCHIES

Companies seem to go through an irreversible life course that leads them towards specialization, complexity and functional parochialism. However hard a business tries to avoid the situation developing, the entrepreneurial start of the business, where practically everyone can do any of the necessary tasks within it, slowly evolves into discrete functions. As functions clone staff together over the years, the rigid development of formal functional structures leads them to become fortresses, the contents of which become the jealously guarded property of the occupants. Inside each fortress, allegiances are high and people speak their own language: a mechanism enabling them to spot intruders and confuse communication.

Organizations are hierarchical, although the transactions and workflow that provide services and products to customers take a horizontal path through the business. The traditional management structure causes managers to put functional needs above those of the multi-functional processes to which their departments contribute. This results in departments competing for resources and blaming one another for any of the company's inexplicable and continuing failures to meet or exceed current customers' needs efficiently.

In highly functional organizations, the different lines of command inside the 'functional silos' create conflicting priorities along multi-functional processes. The performance measures are functional and tend to make functions compete, often at the expense of the customers. There is poor end-to-end visibility of what drives what inside the business. In these circumstances, management loses confidence in the decision support information if it is based on mirroring the functional structures.

## ABM VIEW OF PROCESSES

Internally, the delivery of products and services to customers is the end result of co-ordinated activities by different groups working within the business. A process can be identified at many different scales. At the two ends of the scale we could have the process of building a ship, and the process of authorizing an invoice for pay-

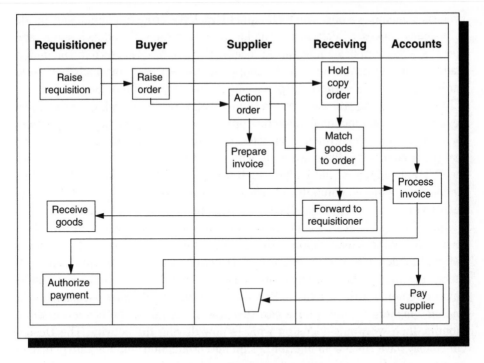

**Figure 5.7** The purchasing process

ment. Conventionally, a process is defined as a set of linked activities across a number of departments. The 'purchasing process' in Figure 5.7 is a typical example.

A list of all the activities found in an ABM analysis may be interesting in its own right, but the primary objective should be to examine all or part of the company's processes to develop implementation plans to improve efficiency and effectiveness. In overall terms, a key driver for change could be that costs must reduce while simultaneously improving quality and customer service.

A fundamental requirement for success of any process improvement programme is the notion of internal customers and suppliers working together in cross-functional processes. An ABM database of activities showing the activities in processes provides this perspective and is an objective basis for:

- understanding any current failures to meet external customers' needs;
- challenging the existing output or levels of service, both externally and internally
- evaluating the benefits of improvements of methods
- understanding cross-functional organizational relationships
- understanding the interactions within multi-functional processes
- identifying and evaluating systems opportunities.

Process mapping is a powerful technique to track the cross-functional flow inside a business process. Such maps quickly highlight failure feedback loops and potential over-complication within a process. The emphasis needs to be on understanding the interaction between the people and the processes in which they work, particularly the points where the processes cross functional boundaries.

Process mapping will also raise a number of issues concerning conventional departmental and functional budgeting procedures. In a typical budget statement for a Purchasing department, extracted from the monthly accounts, one finds that the accounts headings are to do with the resources that go into the department. The headings would include such things as staff costs, travel, telephone, stationery, premises, computer charges and so on. However, the ABM activity analysis raises questions about the type of activities and why they exist.

One of the activities of a Purchasing department is 'assessing needs'. This involves deciding which supplier should quote for the component. The process defines how activities in one department are driven by the outputs from another. If there were no new parts coming from the Design department, then there would be no requirement for the activity in Purchasing. If the activity were associated with finding suppliers or prices for a part that was on its third modification in three months, then we would focus on what is now driving the activity. The Design Office may have rushed an inferior design into production, and the rate of design change may reflect putting the subsequent problems and warranty claims right.

A key aspect of ABM is the emphasis that is placed on achieving a process perspective of the organization and constructing the model in a way that focuses effort on finding ways to improve processes.

## TRADITIONAL VIEW OF VALUE ADDED AND NON-VALUE ADDED

In books and articles, we find the terms value added (VA) and non-value added (NVA) used regularly to separate out those activities that are good for the business from those that are not. From these categories, we would learn that creating scrap is bad, that checking is bad, and so forth. However, the terms VA and NVA provide too coarse a definition of activities in the business, as the subtleties of how failures occur in processes and the impact of customer behaviours are largely invisible.

At a personal level, using the terms 'VA' and 'NVA' can be counterproductive when trying to analyse what is going on when talking to staff. If a situation is found where people are struggling against the vagaries of a process failure, then it is hardly motivating to tell someone that for the last five years their job has been entirely non-value-adding. The nature of process failures is that people do not come to work to cause them, but have to deal with the consequences of failures, usually originating upstream in the process.

44

## ABM VIEW OF TYPES OF ACTIVITY

We have found that it is more enlightening to have three categories we call *core*, *support* and *diversionary*. These terms are defined as follows:

- Core activities use specific skills and expertise and add real value to the business. Core activities are those that provide a necessary service to internal or external customers.
- Support activities make it possible for core activities to take place. For example, a salesperson's time spent negotiating with a customer is a core activity. The travelling time to get to the customer is support.
- Diversionary activities are caused by a process failure somewhere in the organization. Such activities include correcting errors, chasing other groups for information, resolving queries, and so forth. Diversionary activities have many causes, including, for example:
  - inadequate training
  - inadequate tools, procedures and systems
  - poor documentation
  - poor communications
  - poor quality suppliers
  - conflicting functional objectives and performance measures
  - inadequate understanding of customer needs
  - poor customer behaviours.

Poor efficiency and effectiveness can only be eliminated by isolating the root cause of the problem. Frequently, failures cascade through a number of sections, picking up further diversionary activity and therefore costs. By identifying the source of failure and the associated diversionary activity costs, a key outcome should be to change the mix of core, support and diversionary activity within each area of the business. The requirement is to place more emphasis on core activity in order to enhance service quality, and so avoid diversionary activity elsewhere.

An ABM database of activities identified to processes can be coded in order to show the proportions of core, support and diversionary activity as they track through processes. In a typical example, a process started with poor order specification. The effect was compounded as each department attempted to overcome the difficulties created by every department upstream in the process. The delays created pressure from customers, leading to short-term prioritizing of manufacturing schedules and assembly, and excessive overtime working to meet deadlines. The final symptom that highlighted the crisis arose when Production attempted to overcome the backlog of late deliveries. Working from pre-design sketches, Production converted a whole-order quantity of raw material into piece parts

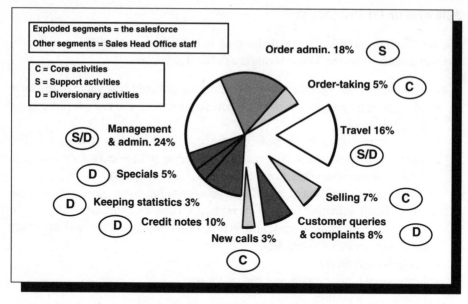

**Figure 5.8** Use of time in a sales process

(aluminium vehicle panels). The customer, on visiting the plant, while delighted that the delivery dates would be met, was curious to know why the specification ordered was not being adhered to. Only a large discount persuaded the customer to take the vehicles as manufactured.

The vagaries of process failure are always around us. Parts do not fit together every time on assembly, invoices have mistakes on them, specifications are incomplete, the computer breaks down, the materials are often inferior, and things just keep letting us down. The processes we are using are not capable of doing the job. And if the process is not capable, then despite our best efforts our output will be of inferior quality. Only by working on the process can it become capable, and its results stable and predictable.

Figure 5.8 shows an example of how the salesforce and Sales Head Office administration department of a manufacturer of office equipment used their time. It was found that only 15 per cent of the whole department's activity was devoted to customer contact. For a typical salesperson, the core activity of 'selling' occupied only 50 per cent of the time spent with customers. The remainder was spent on a diversionary activity, dealing with queries and complaints about delivery performance. Other activities in Head Office – such as credit notes, special invoices, keeping statistics on the problems – and a substantial proportion of management and administration was driven by the same problems. Not surprisingly, the salesforce had little time to spend on new calls to win new customers.

When the process was investigated, each link in the chain pointed to another link as the cause. The atmosphere was one of finding other departments to blame. In this case, striving for functional effectiveness was the underlying root cause of the problem. Functional measures were driving everyone's behaviour. The sales-force was measured on numbers of orders sent in, with month-end panics being the norm. Production ran larger than necessary batches in order to improve machine running-time utilization. Distribution's standard costing variances were reduced by running full loads every time, even if this meant changing customer delivery dates. No end-to-end process measures were in place that related to the processes' ability to satisfy customers at lowest unit cost to the business.

By identifying the root causes of poor delivery performance, a substantial pro-portion of the salesforce's time was released, allowing it to focus on winning more orders. Time was also saved in sales administration, some taken as a cost saving, while some was redeployed into dealer support, handling increased volumes and a new task of telesales.

ABM is crucial in quantifying the process perspective, including the subtle nature of the activities being performed.

## TRADITIONAL VIEW OF BUDGETING

A magazine article discussed how new parents should budget for their newborn baby. The article suggested that parents should budget for functional warm- and cool-weather clothes – at least 20 outfits, 10 newborn undershirts, 15 pairs of socks, and 24 diapers or nappies. On top of these, they should have baby wipes for all-purpose cleaning up, a sturdy big bag, preferably canvas, a baby sling, car seat, cream for rashes, and finally a rocking chair – for simply sitting and nursing during the day. In this context, planning ahead to divide and reallocate scarce resources makes sense. The baby is coming, the situation is inevitable, and its minimum needs must be met. The situation is not dissimilar to planning a new building project. Materials have to be obtained, in the right sequence, and timing is critical.

However, the budgeting process in organizations that results in a monthly set of figures showing budgeted and actual expenditure on resources does not connect with the tangible activities that are performed to provide products and services to customers. 'What is causing resources to be used?' and 'Are they being used effec-tively?' are questions that are not asked during the budgeting process or answered in the monthly reports. The annual budgeting process is often the only attempt by management to plan for the future. At a minimum, it is accepted with reluctance; at worst, it is an excuse to play an extended game of bidding for more cash than is needed in order to end up with less than is vital.

The frustration of the budgeting cycle starts with some sort of strategic plan issued by the Board. However, functions are focused on short-term objectives, so their own sets of objectives tend to have no visible links to show the impact on other functions. The plan is translated under the headings that Finance recognize, such as 'people costs', 'equipment' and so on. These headings are the resources required so that work can be done. The functional budgets are consolidated to company level using the same input resource headings.

Usually, the consolidated totals are more than the Board expected, so a cycle of intensive negotiation and compromise starts in order to achieve acceptable budgets. The articulate and politically astute functional managers tend to do well in these situations. Finally, Finance divides the acceptable total number by 12 and issues departmental monthly budgets. Each month, the accounts are issued and departments are asked to explain their 'VARS', the difference between actual and budget for the month – something the astute manager can do quite easily. Cross-charges and reconciliation queries start to cloud reality. The game for the new budget year is now fully operational.

The conventional budgeting process is fundamentally flawed. Although the budget should be a reflection of the costs to execute and deliver the plan to take the whole business forward, the budgeting process is actioned by inviting each separate function to make bids for resources. The budgeting process also ignores cross-functional processes, and the fact that much activity in one function is driven by the actions in others. Much of managers' budgets can be outside their control. Cross-charges are an inferior method to make some attempt to link services from one department to another, but the underlying drivers of the activities are never the focus of a meaningful discussion between the parties, who are generally at loggerheads over cross-charges.

The budget is expressed as inputs: the resources needed to do something. However, the result of the activities is outputs, the things that impact on internal and, finally, external customers. These key relationships are never expressed in 'budgets'. The key measure should be: 'What did we get for the money?' However, the measure defaults to being: 'Did you meet budget?' Success is seen as meeting budget, rather than achieving the desired outcome from the resources devoted to achieving it. Budgets extrapolated from the past have no bearing on the plans for the future. Lacking a link between activities, volumes and product and customer mix, managers fall back on just adding 10 per cent in the hope they might get 5 per cent.

## ABM VIEW OF BUDGETING

Activity Based Budgeting can be categorized as looking at costs in the reverse direction from conventional budgeting. Rather than determining resources (ledger line items), ABB starts with forecasting the number of products and services, the number of customers and level of service to them. ABB then identifies the activities that would be needed, and finally identifies the resources required so the new level of activities can take place.

An ABM model is built by working forwards from resources to activities and on to products, services and customers. This provides the base data for ABB. Stripped to its basics, ABB starts with a knowledge of which activities are related to, say, a particular product, service or customer. The relationship between a product and the activities to produce it is called the *driver* of the activity. If the product were an insurance policy sold via a call-centre operation, then the activity of 'sell policy' would have a driver and driver volume called 'number of policies sold'. By forecasting the volume of policies to be sold in the future budget period, we can derive the level of activity required to service the demand. This assumes the current service level using the current methods, both of which could be changed by management decision or process re-design.

Having determined what products or services will be provided, and the quantity of each activity that will be consumed, the next step is to determine what resources will be required. The costs of each activity will have been determined in the ABM model by analysing and assigning the resources in the ledger down to activities. Activity costs naturally include the salary costs of the people doing the work, but also the costs of the space they occupy, the IT they use, the stationery they consume, and so forth. Having determined the likely level of activities required to provide the services, ABB works backwards from activities to the resources which the activities consume using the relationship between resources and activities. If the level of physical activity is forecast to increase by, say, 20 per cent, then the assumption is that salary costs will rise by the same proportion, as more people are needed. If the accommodation costs have been assigned to activities on the basis of area, then the new level of activities is assumed to require more space in which to do the work, based on the same proportions of space to activity level that were used in the model. For activities such as 'driving a vehicle', an increase in activity levels implies an increase in the number of vehicles. Where a computer terminal is used, then at some point more terminals will be needed.

In reality, the relationships between product, activities and resources are not so simple. Some costs may be semi-variable or even fixed in the forecast scenario. For example, although training costs will have been assigned to the activities of people in the business who receive training, only parts of the total Training department's costs, such as the trainers themselves, would vary as other activities in the business increase. The Training department's building would remain at the same cost. Other costs would have been assigned, but there exists spare capacity that can be used when volumes somewhere else increase. Some costs, such as year-end financial reporting, have almost no relationship to the volumes of products being produced.

All these factors must be taken into account when calculating the budget, based on the products or services being provided and the number and types of customers being serviced. By thinking through the logical relationships and making the necessary adjustments depending on the cost types, ABB traces activities back to ledger accounts from the starting point of products, services and customers.

Although not quite at the 'touch of a button', we could predict a significant reduction in organizational angst and lead time by using Activity Based Budgeting.

## KEY POINTS

- Traditional product costing relies on using an Overhead Recovery Rate (ORR) to allocate overheads to products, causing high distortions to product costs. In ABM, the indirect and overhead costs associated with each product are determined accurately for each product.

- In traditional accounting we find the term 'gross margin', defined as the revenue minus the direct costs. The issue is that we do not know, other than at the overall company level, whether this contribution has any bearing whatsoever on the real overheads involved in producing each particular product or serving each customer. ABM analysis uncovers the actual indirect and overhead costs associated with producing each product and servicing customers. Revenue minus the actual product costs gives the ABM Product Contribution. Revenue minus the real costs of the products the customer is ordering and minus the real cost of servicing the customer gives the ABM Customer Contribution. ABM Contributions are an appropriate basis on which to compare products and customers.

- In the accounts, costs are expensed under headings such as 'salaries' and lumped together as business overheads. This simple categorization of diverse activities obscures the rich diversity of tasks being undertaken in a business to serve many purposes. In ABM, the diverse costs and activities are categorized as *frontline, internal service, sustaining* or *infrastructure*, so we can understand what is happening inside the business.

- In highly functional organizations there is poor end-to-end visibility of what drives what inside the business. In these circumstances, management loses confidence in the decision support information if it is based on mirroring the functional structures. A fundamental requirement for success of any process improvement programme is the notion of internal customers and suppliers working together in cross-functional processes. An ABM database of activities showing the activities in processes provides this perspective.

- Value added (VA) and non-value added (NVA) are terms that have been used to separate out those activities that are good for the business from those that are not. These terms are too coarse a definition to expose the subtleties of how failures occur in processes, and the impact of customer behaviours is largely invisible. It is more enlightening to have three categories that are called *core*, *support* and *diversionary*. In ABM, quantifying the process perspective by including the subtle nature of the activities being performed identifies the benefits of making process improvements and changing customer behaviours.

- However, the budgeting process in organizations that results in a monthly set of figures showing budgeted and actual expenditure on resources does not connect with the tangible activities that are performed to provide products and services to customers. Activity Based Budgeting (ABB) looks at costs in the reverse direction from conventional budgeting. Rather than determining resources (ledger line items), ABB starts with forecasting the number of products and services, the number of customers and level of service to them. ABB then identifies the activities that would be needed and finally identifies the resources required so that the new level of activities can take place.

# Part II
# ABM in Practice

# 6 The ABM flow of costs

ABM takes a more natural view of the real world. Bearing in mind the ABM framework definitions set out in Chapter 5, we will now show how an ABM approach was applied in a simple catering business. This business has a conventional restaurant to serve customers who eat in, and it has another source of revenue from providing meals to a number of local retirement homes. The overall flow of costs is shown in Figure 6.1.

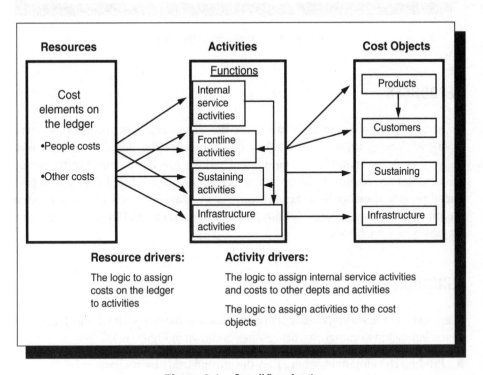

**Figure 6.1   Overall flow of costs**

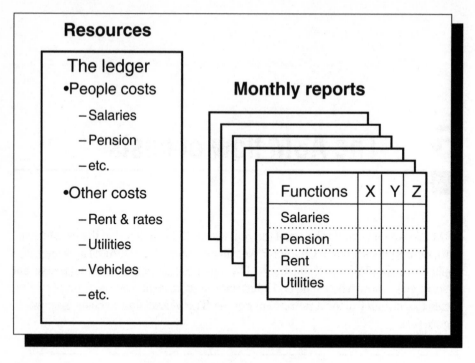

**Figure 6.2**   Resources on the ledger

## RESOURCES

From the Finance department, we know the 'resources' used in the restaurant business. Among these are the salary costs, rent for the building, utility costs, delivery vehicles, rental for the equipment and the raw ingredients for the meals. These costs are found on the ledger as shown on Figure 6.2. Finance also produced reports showing how these resources were used in each department each month, but the departments did not feel that the reports told them how effective the business actually was.

## FUNCTIONS

The restaurant has a conventional organizational structure with various functions. The relationship to categories of activities is shown in Figure 6.3:

- Product Development, where they design and trial new recipes.
- Marketing, where they prepare adverts for the local press and radio

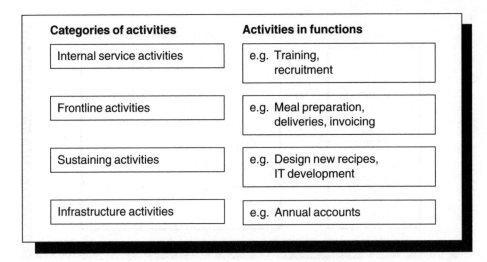

**Figure 6.3** Functions and activity categories

- Finance, where they process receipts from the restaurant, invoice the retirement homes, pay suppliers, keep track of items on the ledger and prepare the statutory accounts
- Purchasing, which buys the ingredients
- the Preparation department, where they cut the meat and clean and prepare the vegetables
- the Kitchen, where the meals are made
- the Servers, who take orders and deliver meals to the tables
- the Delivery Service, which takes meals to the retirement homes.

In the ABM approach, the business was interested in what people were doing, and for what purposes the activities were being carried out. Also, it was interested in what caused the activities to change, either up or down, as this had an impact on the resources that were needed in the future. Finally, understanding product and customer profitability would guide decisions about the direction that the business should be taking.

## ACTIVITIES AND DRIVERS

Each of the departments listed their activities. Next, the costs on the ledger, the *resources*, were assigned to the activities. To do this, they used a particular type of *cost driver*. A cost driver is any variable whose change in frequency causes an increase or decrease in a cost or activity. A *resource driver* is the type of cost driver

57

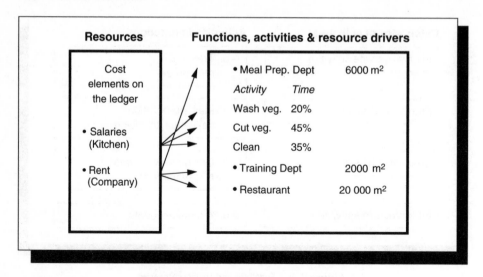

**Figure 6.4**    Assigning resources to activities

that is used to assign the resources that are consumed by a particular activity to that activity. As an example, when assigning the cost of a resource such as salaries to an activity, the amount of effort required to perform that activity had to be identified. Here, the resource driver called 'headcount' was used. In other words, the analysis had to find out how many people worked on each activity. This is also equivalent to working out the percentage of time everyone in a department spends on each of the activities in the department. For the cost of the rent, the space occupied was used to assign costs on the basis of the area each department occupied. The link from resources to activities using resource drivers is shown in Figure 6.4. For each of the activities, thought was given to the question of what changes the level of activity. The volume of the cost driver that influences the activity changes the level of the activity. These are known as *activity drivers*. The classification of *frontline* activities was introduced. These are activities to do with making the product or dealing in some way with customers. For many of the frontline activities associated with producing products, the cost drivers are simple volumes of something. For example, the activity of 'cut vegetable' would be driven by the number of vegetables to be cut. Likewise, the activity of 'prepare invoices' would be driven by the number of invoices to be prepared.

Other activities are close to the frontline but are known as *internal service*. Here, there are no direct relationships to the product or customer, but there is a relationship to the frontline activities. For example, in the Personnel department, the training costs mainly varied depending on the training days received by other departments as shown on Figure 6.5. However, before assigning frontline activity

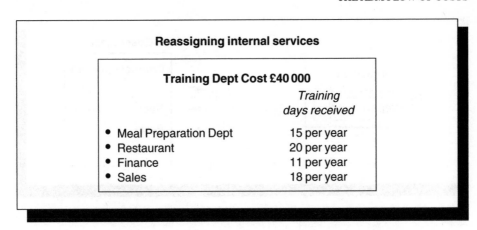

**Reassigning internal services**

**Training Dept Cost £40 000**

*Training days received*

- Meal Preparation Dept     15 per year
- Restaurant     20 per year
- Finance     11 per year
- Sales     18 per year

**Figure 6.5**    Reassigning an internal service (for example, training)

costs to the products, channels and customers, we need to calculate the amount of internal service costs that have to be assigned to the frontline activities. Training is given to people in all the departments. The next step calculated the proportion of training given to each department, and then the department's training costs were assigned to the activities within the department.

There are often several cost drivers for a single activity, particularly if the activity is a high-level one. The activity 'contact suppliers' could be caused by late deliveries that need chasing, or placing new orders, or simply discussing new types of materials they are offering. To arrive at a better understanding of the cause-and-effect relationship, the high-level activity would need to be broken down to a lower level to see if there exists a dominant cost driver that can be used. If all the cost drivers are relevant, then you need a more detailed analysis, which in turn increases the complexity of the ABM model.

By forecasting the volume of the significant cost drivers and relating this to the activities they drive, a new value for the level of resource can be determined. This is the basis of Activity Based Budgeting. For example, the relationship between training and other activities in the business is now known. As the business was forecast to grow, the impact on training resources could be predicted with greater accuracy.

## PRODUCTS, CHANNELS AND CUSTOMERS

The main object of the ABM exercise was to cost the products (meals), the channels of supply (the restaurant and delivery service) and the customers (by category). The products, channels and customers are known as the *cost objects*.

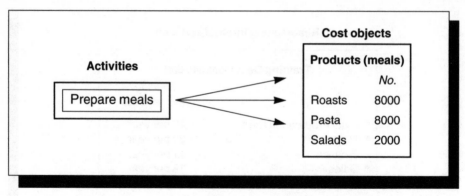

**Figure 6.6**  Assigning activities to cost objects (for example, products)

The relationship between activities and the cost objects, such as products, is found by analysing the activity drivers. Activity drivers are the means for assigning a costed activity to the object that is consuming that particular activity. Here, for instance, if the costed activity is 'prepare meals', and you want to establish product costs, the activity driver called 'volume of meals' (by each type) might be appropriate, as shown on Figure 6.6.

Although separate driver definitions have been used in this restaurant example, such as resource driver and activity driver, various books, articles in journals and ABM software packages from various suppliers often use the single term 'cost driver'. Using the specific terms makes it clear which step in the assignment process is being handled in the ABM model. The business wanted to find out the cost of the products in two major categories: meals eaten in and those delivered. This calculation was taken up to the point where both types of meal were ready in the kitchen. The raw materials for each of the meals were known from the recipes and the total quantity of meals prepared. The *direct* activities of cooking the different meals were easy to find out. There were *indirect* activities, such as inspecting and cleaning the ingredients. There were *overhead* activities in the Purchasing department, which obtained the materials from suppliers. The indirect and overhead activities needed more thought before assigning the activity costs to the products.

When you take an ABM view of an organization, the traditional classifications of indirect and overhead costs now seem strange. In traditional accounting, the indirect and overhead costs are often treated as an amorphous lump of expense that has little relationship to direct costs. The basic difference between overhead costs and direct costs is that it is more difficult to see the connection between overhead costs and the products. This may only be a small point, but it is one of the fundamental differences between traditional accounting and the ABM approach that has caused significant problems in the many other ways in which costs are treated.

Next, the restaurant business wanted to know the costs of the two channels of supply to customers: meals eaten in the restaurant, and meals delivered to retirement homes. This would bring in the activities of taking orders through the two channels: serving the meals inside, and delivering the meals outside. Also, the assets were used differently. The restaurant used a large proportion of the building, while the delivery service used all the vehicles.

Finally, the restaurant wanted to know the costs of customers. At this point, it considered how it wanted to analyse customer costs. It thought of a number of options:

1. all the restaurant customers as one group, and all the retirement homes as another group.
2. the restaurant as two groups – one group of customers who used the 'Quick-Meal' service, and those that used the 'Full-Menu' service
3. the retirement homes divided into two groups, depending on the levels of service provided
4. each retirement home as a separate customer.

It went for (2) and (3), which gave a total of four separate customer cost objects.

The decision on cost objects now determined how other departments' costs had to be treated in the model. In the Finance department, some activities were concerned with handling cash and credit card payments from the restaurant, while others were concerned with raising invoices and chasing payments from the retirement homes. Activity drivers, such as 'number of credit card payments', were split into the numbers from each part of the restaurant, as shown in Figure

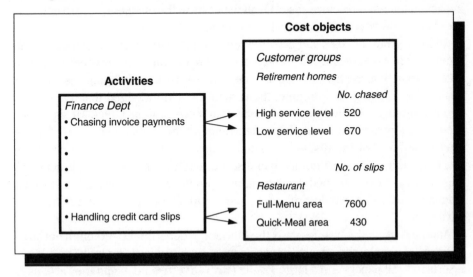

**Figure 6.7**    Assigning activities to cost objects (for example, customers)

6.7. Other overhead activities, such as the Sales department, now had to be considered for the first time. The Sales activities of visiting current customers to talk about issues to do with the retirement homes were assigned on the basis of the levels of service: number of visits. Some Marketing and menu design activities were associated with certain retirement homes and not others.

## INFRASTRUCTURE AND SUSTAINING COSTS

So far, the restaurant had analysed all the costs – direct, indirect and overhead – that could be assigned using drivers to its products, channels and customers. There were still a number of costs and activities that had not been assigned at this stage.

In the Finance department, there were some activities that were necessary in order to prepare the annual accounts. The external auditors also charged for their services. Some management time was taken up by having to read and act on changes to legislation concerning food preparation and handling. Also, a government department required the restaurant to submit a number of returns on a monthly basis concerning various aspects of its business. All these types of cost and activity are classified as *infrastructure*. They are costs that arise because it is a business, and do not vary as a result of product or customer types and volumes.

The ABM Customer Contribution (revenue minus actual product and customer costs) has to pay for the infrastructure costs. If the number of products and overall sales volume of the products increased or decreased, then this had little or no impact on the infrastructure costs. Of all the costs in the business, infrastructure is the closest one gets to the notion of fixed costs.

Another group of costs and activities were in place to ensure the business had a future. These were the *sustaining* costs. New product development was seen as essential. The restaurant had to keep pace with the changing tastes of its customers. Looking back in time, the restaurant acknowledged that a few years ago it only had a limited range of meals that were sold as 'Quick-Meals'. Since then, it had introduced a completely new range of meals that now featured in the 'Full-Menu' part of the restaurant. The extension of its business into providing meals for the retirement homes had also occurred in the last year. It acknowledged that if it ever stopped developing new products and services, then it would stagnate: customers would drift away, and competitors would gain a permanent advantage.

Another cost in the business was the Marketing department. Although not large in terms of people, the advertising costs were high. Advertising took the form of inserts in local papers and a large *Yellow Pages* advertisement, and they also used the local radio station in two ways: radio ads either just promoted the restaurant's

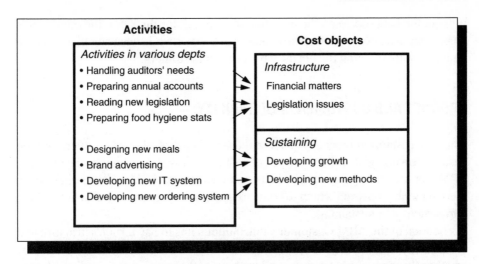

**Figure 6.8** Assigning activities to cost objects (for example, sustaining and infrastructure)

name in a general way, or advertised special meal extravaganza events that were expected to create a peak level of customers. Some of these costs were to do with enhancing the brand – the restaurant's name – and thus ensured a steady flow of new customers. Other costs were very specific to certain products – the specials – and groups of customers – those that came to the 'Murder & Mystery' evenings.

Expenditure on IT had taken place some years ago. The depreciation costs were treated as internal service, and were assigned to all the activities that used IT in some form. However, there were some costs being incurred to develop a complete replacement for their IT system: not only a faster suite of programmes that would run on new hardware, but also a new telephone ordering system that relied on voice recognition to place orders. The new investment it was making in IT was seen as essential to secure the business's long-term future. Assigning activities to infrastructure and sustaining cost objects is shown in Figure 6.8.

The ABM Customer Contribution (revenue minus actual product and customer costs) has to pay for the sustaining costs. Management has a choice about whether or not to invest in these areas. Making a cost reduction would leave more of the contribution available as profit, but risks the future of the business. Increasing investment in sustaining might not secure the return that is required. Where shareholders are involved, they will be happy to leave retained profit in the business as long as they are assured that the money will work for them in the future.

The management judgement and decisions on what to spend on sustaining are therefore different to the tasks and decisions concerned with the everyday business of preparing meals and serving customers. For the former, the requirement is to get the best return on the investment, whereas, for the latter, the emphasis is on becoming more cost-effective at today's processes while ensuring that as a minimum they are meeting the needs of the current customers.

## PRODUCT AND CUSTOMER PROFITABILITY

Once the restaurant business had found the real cost of all of its products and the costs of serving all its different types of customer, it was then able to calculate the ABM Contributions from its products and customers. ABM Contributions are a more equitable basis on which to compare profitability, as the costs do not include infrastructure or sustaining.

The total of the ABM Customer Contributions has to pay for infrastructure and sustaining costs, and anything left over is profit. The restaurant was keen to know whether there were any products and customers that were only providing a low or negative ABM Contribution. If there were, then it would have to take some action to overcome the problem.

The hook curve of cumulative ABM Product Contribution found a number of products where the actual costs to produce them were not covered by the income from the products. The 'Quick-Meal' range of Hungarian salads had a number of high-cost ingredients and took a long time to prepare. Also, the training costs were high, as they required some particular skills. Raising the price to give a positive ABM Product Contribution was not seen as an option, as the salads would appear disproportionately highly priced compared to similar meals in the salad range. A trial at a higher price had only resulted in the salads being left on display at the end of the day. Hungarian salads were dropped from the range.

The hook curve of cumulative ABM Customer Contribution indicated that the high level of service given to a certain type of retirement home was the reason for them being negative contributors. At the product level, the contributions were positive. The issue was really one of increasing the volume to these customers. At the time of the analysis, the group of homes was deciding whether to outsource all of its meals service. The restaurant decided to continue the relationship without a price rise, as the prize was to complete the trial at one home and then win the contract for all six homes.

In the 'Full-Menu' part of the restaurant, the ABM product and customer contributions were both high. The restaurant decided to enhance the service level provided to these customers, as it judged it would then get a higher 'star' rating, which in turn would draw in more customers. Although the customers it would then attract would be expecting an even higher-quality meal, management felt it could adjust prices to retain the same contribution levels.

## ATTRIBUTE ANALYSIS

Due to changes in legislation, the restaurant had to determine which activities were concerned with directly handling food, and which activities needed temperature-controlled environments. As the activities were not always exactly the same for both categories, it was necessary to use two attributes: 'handling' and 'temperature control'. By adding these attributes against the appropriate activities, it was possible to extract all the relevant activities from the ABM model's database. Other linked information was also extracted, such as the department where the activity took place, and the activity cost.

## PROCESSES AND PROCESS IMPROVEMENT

So far, the analysis of activities had been undertaken within the departments and functions. The restaurant realized that it would be useful to see how various processes tracked through the business, crossing functional boundaries. The key processes were defined as:

- Process No. 1 – developing new business opportunities
- Process No. 2 – satisfying current customer demand
- Process No. 3 – cash collections.

Each of these processes had major inputs from parts of one or two departments, and a number of smaller inputs from peripheral departments. Using another attribute, 'process', the activities were flagged with a process number, such as (No. 2). The total activity list, with all the constituent elements of costs, was extracted from the database.

From the analysis, it became clear that there were opportunities to reduce the costs through improvements in the methods that were being used. The impact of the changes could be simulated in the model, and the effect on the ABM Contributions calculated. This gave support to the argument in favour of making a number of process changes. During the analysis of activities, it was noticed that most of the activities were *core* to the business. The core activities used the skills of the people and added directly to moving the business forward. Typical of these were 'prepare ingredients', 'negotiate with new customer', 'prepare bills' and so forth.

However, some activities were really to do with a failure in the process, or were caused by some customer actions or behaviours that created unwanted costs in the business. One activity was 're-cook meal'. This occurred when the head waiter felt that the quality of the meal was inferior and refused to serve it to a customer. Another activity was 'rush extra meals to retirement home'. This occurred when the restaurant had taken down the telephone order incorrectly. Another activity was 'chase payments'. This occurred when a retirement home failed to comply with the agreed credit period. All these activities were *diversionary*. The activity had to be carried out, but it diverted people away from their core activities. The diversionary activities could be avoided if the process was made more robust or the customer behaviour changed.

As the restaurant felt that an analysis of the core and diversionary activities would be useful as a way to focus on reducing the costs of its operations, it decided to re-visit the activity analysis so it could add further attributes. At this point it realized that in some departments the level of the activity was too high. Further discussions with the people in the department enabled them to break down the high-level activities into more detail that brought out the different types of activity. Once the model was refreshed with the additional activity data, the attributes for type of activity were added.

The range of attributes shown in Figure 6.9 provided the means to analyse the business in a very insightful manner. The process and activity analysis gave a completely new view of the business. People working in a department could now see the whole process, and the causes and effects of both failures in the process and customer behaviours. What was particularly noticeable was that coming up with actions to reduce or eliminate the diversionary activities and redirect these efforts to additional core activities would be the quickest route to growing the business without taking on additional resources. Effectively reducing the unit costs allowed increased volumes and enhanced services to be handled without increasing total costs.

The restaurant now had a complete ABM model. This is shown in Figure 6.10. The resources were assigned to the activities using resource drivers. The internal service activities were assigned to other activities, and the activity costs assigned to the cost objects using activity drivers. By introducing the revenue, the model calculated product and customer profitability (ABM Product and Customer

| Activity | Process | Cost type | Activity type | Diversionary cause |
|----------|---------|-----------|---------------|--------------------|
| A1 | Proc. No. 2 | Frontline | Core | — |
| A2 | Proc. No. 1 | Support | Diversionary | Process failure |
| A3 | Proc. No. 2 | Frontline | Diversionary | Customer behaviour |

**Figure 6.9**   Activity attributes

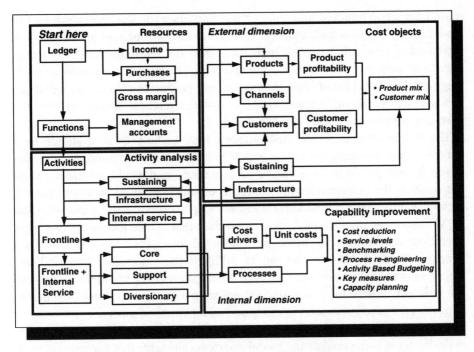

**Figure 6.10** The complete ABM model

Contributions). By using attributes, activities were analysed to provide a focus on aspects of the business where it was advantageous to improve its effectiveness.

## EMBEDDING THE MODEL

Creating the model was only the start of using ABM as the ongoing approach to running the business. Two key aspects had to be considered:

1. how to keep the model up to date
2. how to ensure the information was used.

The model had to be a credible reflection of reality. By this we mean that the model had to be accepted throughout the business as containing data that was relevant to the way work was being done. As activities and processes changed, then this had to be reflected in the model. As the ledger costs changed, this also had to be included, and likewise the driver volumes.

The model did not have to be an exact replica of either the business or the management accounts. However, the notion of materiality had to be considered before changing the structure or data content of the model. If the activities were

67

moved from one function into another function, then the cost outputs from the model would not materially change. If, say, the turnover of staff in one function increased significantly to a new high level, then the recruitment activity would have to be assigned on a new basis, but only if the recruitment costs were material (high) in the overall list of costs. A range of new products or the introduction of a new segment of customer types would be material, as these would not have any costs assigned to them in the current model.

The frequency with which ABM models have to be refreshed should be a commonsense decision. A monthly update of ledger costs and monthly collection of activity data would be tiresome for all concerned, and would not make a large difference to the outputs from the model. The model might be 'accurate', but the irksome nature of the refreshing process would give everyone the impression that ABM was just another monthly burden on their time. Once the model produced useful outputs that management and staff used to improve the business, then people welcomed ABM as an aid to fulfilling their normal responsibilities. Decisions were better, and the results of the decisions were tracked through into the business. Where there was uncertainty as to a particular course of action to take, then the proposed scenario was tested using the ABM model.

To achieve this level of embedding requires that specific ABM expertise exists in the business to manipulate the model and extract insights that line management would not see in the normal course of business. Line managers will be able to raise questions about the business that can be answered through the model without having to be ABM model experts themselves. Embedding is thus a process of establishing ABM as a natural way of understanding the business, and acting on the information ABM provides.

## KEY POINTS

- A *cost driver* is any variable whose change in frequency causes an increase or decrease in a cost or activity. A *resource driver* is the type of cost driver that is used to assign the resources that are consumed by a particular activity to that activity. An *activity driver* is the type of cost driver that influences the level of an activity. Activity drivers are used to assign activities to other activities (such as training assigned to those being trained) and to assign activities to cost objects (for example, sales visits assigned to customers being visited).

- The products, channels and customers are known as the *cost objects*. The relationship between activities and the cost objects, such as products, is found by analysing the activity drivers. Activity drivers are the means of assigning a costed activity to the object that is consuming that particular activity.

- By adding attributes against the appropriate activities, it is possible to extract all the relevant activities from an ABM model's database that share the same attribute. Attributes can be any characteristic of interest. Typically, identifying which process the activity is in is a useful attribute.

- The attributes of *core*, *support* or *diversionary* provide the means to understand the nature of the work being done.

- The process and activity analysis provides a completely new view of a business. People working in a department can then see the whole process, and the causes and effects of both failures in the process and customer behaviours.

- An ABM model has to be a credible reflection of reality so that the model will be accepted throughout the business as containing data that is relevant to the way work is being done. The model does not have to be an exact replica of either the business or the management accounts. However, the notion of materiality has to be considered before changing the structure or data content of the model.

- The frequency with which ABM models have to be refreshed should be a commonsense decision. A monthly update of ledger costs and monthly collection of activity data would be tiresome for all concerned, and would not make a large difference to the outputs from the model.

- Embedding the model in the business is the process of establishing ABM as a natural way of understanding the business, and acting on the information ABM provides.

# 7 The basic principles of building models

When starting to build ABM models, there are a number of issues to consider before plunging into the detail, which risks never surfacing with a completed model or one that can be refreshed and used continually as a decision support tool. As always, some thought and planning at an early stage will prevent a path being taken that leads to an inefficient model or one that does not cover the business issues ABM was hoping to address. When structuring a model, there are a number of key points to consider.

We will need to start with a schematic plan of the flow of costs in the model. Next, we'll need to understand the general ledger and determine how we will assign costs to activities. We will need to consider the level of detail required during activity data collection and whether we will use attributes to facilitate extracting data of interest to illustrate particular issues.

Cost drivers – both resource and activity – will need to be considered early, as the sources of data may be lacking or difficult to obtain. This will also be part of the discussion concerning how to assign costs to frontline activities, reassign internal service costs to frontline activities, and onwards to products and customers.

We will need to consider how we will show product and customer profitability. Will this be at an individual level, or will we choose product categories or customer segments?

Many useful outputs could be obtained. We need to consider how we will use unit cost data for budgeting or benchmarking, or in simulation models of other scenarios for running the business.

We'll look in depth at each of these considerations.

## THE FLOW OF COSTS IN THE MODEL

An ABM model is a large assignment engine. It moves costs from one entity to another, based on a cascade of assignments. The entities are:

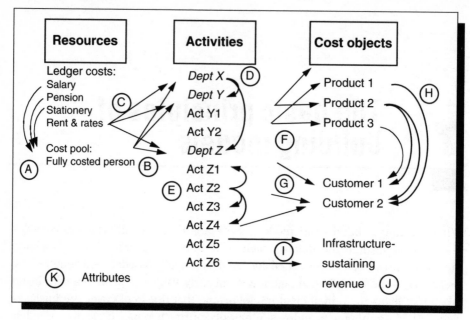

**Figure 7.1** The cascade of assignments in an ABM model

- cost elements in the ledger – the resources so work can take place
- functions, departments, sections and, finally, activities – where the work is done
- cost objects – the products and services, channels of supply, and the customers, the reason why work is done.

The logic is the cost drivers:

- resource drivers, to assign costs to functions, departments, sections or activities
- activity drivers, which assign the costs of activities to other activities or to the cost objects.

The terms 'cost drivers' or just 'drivers' are often used generically, and in this context are used to define the basis of the logic to move one cost from one entity to another. Depending on where you are in the model, they could be specifically a resource driver or an activity driver.

The cascade of assignments is shown in Figure 7.1.

A. Use cost pools to reduce complexity in the model (consolidate a number of cost elements into a 'fully costed person').

B. Assign costs using resource drivers (fully costed person cost pool, on the basis of numbers of people in each department).

C. Assign costs using resource drivers (rent and rates, on the basis of space used in each department).
D. Assign an internal service department's costs to other departments using activity drivers (Training department on the basis of the numbers of people being trained in other departments).
E. Assign some activities to other activities using activity drivers (managing staff on the basis of the percentage of time staff spend on activities in the department).
F. Assign activities (and direct costs) to products using activity drivers.
G. Assign activities to customers using activity drivers.
H. Assign products to customers.
I. Assign infrastructure and sustaining costs and activities to similar cost objects.
J. Add in the revenue by product and customer, and so calculate profitability.
K. Use attributes to add further dimensions of analysis. The attributes can be added to resources, activities and cost objects. Attributes provide a simple mechanism for extracting data from the model.

When planning the construction of a model, it is wise to start with a schematic version drawn on paper showing the logic that will be used to assign resources to activities and activities to cost objects. Also, some thought should be given as to how each part of the model will be structured.

For resources, the structure will generally match the ledger. This is the source of all the costs and the main link to the company's ledger systems. However, if the model is going to consolidate cost elements from the ledger into cost pools, then the basis for this and any assumptions made concerning which cost elements are to be pooled should be clearly noted. At a later date, the assumptions may change, either in the interest of materiality or accuracy, or because 'What if?' scenarios are to be tested.

For activities, there are a number of considerations. The activities can be shown in the model grouped within departments and functions. This would match the organization structure and current boundaries of cost centres shown in the accounts. If the company is keen to have the model show how activities and costs appear within processes, then rather than use process attributes for each activity, the structure of the model can reflect processes and activities assigned to the processes.

As it is simpler to collect activity data by departments rather than by multi-department processes, the model can have two stages. Firstly, resources are assigned to departments, and the department costs assigned to their activities. Secondly, departmental activities are assigned to the processes. The activities now in processes would be assigned to the cost objects.

On the planning schematic, the basis for assigning resources to departments should be shown. These are the resource drivers. For example, the driver could be square metres for accommodation costs, although finding out the actual areas would be part of data collection. Again, any assumptions concerning the application of the drivers should be logged. Accommodation costs may be treated as one grand total to be assigned, or it may be necessary to take the actual costs of each building where there are significant differences between types of buildings. In this case, a two-step process is used, firstly to assign costs to each building, then secondly to assign the building costs to the departments that occupy the buildings.

Prior to collecting activity data, the planning schematic should show, for each department, the level of detail to be collected, whether attributes will be used and, if so, which ones. In some cases, it might be expedient to consider creating a 'common activity dictionary', particularly where the same departments or sections are repeated at a number of locations: for example, a branch network in a number of geographic regions. Before collecting data, it is prudent to test how representative the dictionary will be by trialling it at a single branch before using it to collect data from all branches. Having a common dictionary is very useful where all the branches are to be compared in terms of use of time in relation to each branch's performance. This highlights where best practice might exist which can be implemented across all branches.

It is very easy to become swamped by activity data. The planning schematic should indicate where it is appropriate to collect activity data at either a high level or at a detailed level. For the initial model, whole departments in the infrastructure and sustaining categories would pass as single activities to infrastructure and sustaining cost objects. Internal service departments could be represented as single activities if there were single cost drivers to assign their costs to other departments.

Frontline activities are assigned to cost objects using activity drivers. The activities need only be collected down to a level where a single primary activity driver assigns the costs to the cost objects. Although an activity such as 'visit customers' may have a number of sub-activities that take place during a visit, if they are all triggered by the occurrence of a visit to a customer, then adding all the sub-activities to the model introduces unnecessary complexity.

For cost objects, the primary consideration is to set down on the planning schematic the final definitions of the destinations of all the costs in the model. These can be products or channels or customers, and any combination of the three to any level of detail for which data exists. For example, a bank may want to calculate the profitability of customer segments, such as all those with mortgages, rather than go down to each customer's individual profitability. The latter may be a more important criterion for a utility company that wishes to link customer profitability to data that highlights characteristics of customer behaviour from other sources found by their individual postcode.

For products, the cost objects could be individual contracts for large equipment, such as power generation sets, or it could be segments, such as generators within a particular power range. In a bakery, product cost objects could be by type, such as bread and cakes, or down to every single product. For an insurance company, the channels of supply could be important cost objects. The same product could be sold through the direct call-centre channel as well as through brokers.

An important consideration at the planning stage is to define the sources of activity driver data. Much of the data will come from the company's current transaction files, such as the sales ledger. Other necessary data may be non-existent, such as logs of visits to customers. Knowing this at the planning stage allows more time for data creation in the areas where the driver volumes and proportions by cost object will be assigning significant costs through the model.

## THE GENERAL LEDGER

In many companies, the general ledger will have been around for a long time, and probably in a form that does not lend itself readily to being the start point for an ABM model. The ledger will probably suffer from some or all of the following hindrances:

- The structure has not been reviewed for years.
- Expense headings have proliferated.
- Redundant codes remain.
- The discipline and accuracy of ledger entries is poor.
- Cross-charging obscures any valuable meaning.
- Managers have a low level of ownership of the data posted to their cost centre.

Although it may satisfy the needs of financial accounting, it may be necessary to spend some time cleaning up the ledger if it is to be used as a dependable source of data for an ABM model. The key requirement is to be able to extract costs from the ledger in a way that facilitates making the links between the activities and the ledger costs.

## CATEGORIES OF COSTS AND ACTIVITIES

It is useful if the ABM model can be structured to recognize that all costs and activities fall into one of four categories. As was explained earlier, the categories help us to understand the nature of various costs and activities and how they need to be considered in the short and long term. Let us reprise the definitions.

Some resources are devoted to *frontline* activities, such as making parts or processing customer orders. These activities have a direct cause-and-effect relationship to the cost objects such as products, services, customers or channels.

Some resources are devoted to an *internal service* of other parts of the business. Personnel and Training are a service to parts of the business and so have only an indirect link to the cost objects. The internal service costs and activities are reassigned to the other categories of activities based on a secondary cost driver. For example, training could be reassigned on the basis of the headcount of the other departments that receive training or the training hours devoted to each department.

Some resources are devoted to *sustaining* the future, such as product development, and have no direct link to the cost objects. Sustaining costs should not be assigned to current products or customers when using the data to investigate customer profitability. Current customers have to generate an ABM Customer Contribution that can then be used to pay for sustaining costs. If the sustaining costs were assigned to current products and customers, then either or both could become 'unprofitable' and be dropped. However, the sustaining costs would still remain, as they had no cost driver link to products or customers.

Some resources are devoted to the *infrastructure*, such as running the business, and are independent of business volumes. Statutory accounts, the annual audit, and producing health and safety policies would fall into this category. No cost drivers link to products or customers, and no secondary cost drivers link to any of the other activities. Current customers have to generate an ABM Customer Contribution that has to cover infrastructure costs.

## ASSIGNING COSTS FROM THE GENERAL LEDGER

The general ledger is the source of all the costs that go into the ABM model. The first requirement is to ascertain whether the figures shown in the ledger can be assigned with confidence to the degree of detail that is needed in the model. How the costs are reported in the ledger will determine how much work will have to be done to attribute the right costs to the departments prior to assigning them to activities.

A very simple ledger may only have the costs shown as expenditure types at the highest summary level, some of which are shown in Table 7.1.

The first step would be to assign the total payroll costs to each department. A simple means would be to assign the total payroll based on the headcount in each department. Based on headcount, the departmental payroll costs would not be

**Table 7.1    Example of a simple ledger**

| Expenditure type | Amount |
| --- | --- |
| Payroll | £2 700 000 |
| Travel | £119 000 |
| Rent | £1 000 000 |

accurate, as each department would have different salary rates. Depending on the purpose of the model, this may or may not be a big problem. However, in most organizations the starting point is usually a ledger that has the numbers already broken down in some detail for such costs as payroll, showing costs by functions and departments. The total payroll cost would then be accurate for each department, as it would be based on the actual salaries.

To reduce the model's complexity without loss of accuracy, ledger costs may be consolidated into *cost pools*. A cost pool collects costs together that can be assigned to activities as a single cost element. Cost pools can be created at various organizational levels, as shown in Figure 7.2.

For 'payroll' costs, rather than individually assigning the separate cost elements

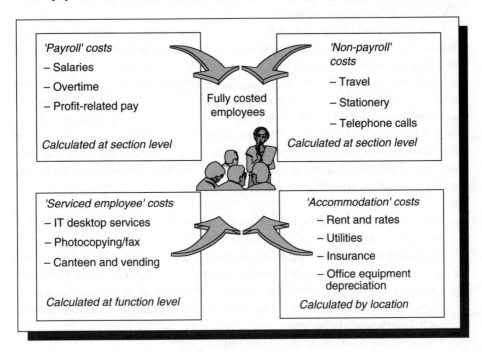

**Figure 7.2    Cost pools**

in the ledger of salaries, overtime and profit-related pay to activities, a single cost pool for each organizational section could be created. It makes more sense to create the 'serviced employee' cost pool at function level. This pool would be assigned to sections in the function based on headcount.

At the lowest organizational unit, say a section, a final cost pool of the 'fully costed employee' would then be assigned to the individual activities in each section.

Where a cost centre manager cannot generally influence costs, then these ledger lines may only appear at the highest level. Accommodation costs could be such an example. Rent could then be assigned to departments on the basis of area occupied.

A key issue when determining how to handle each type of cost in the ledger is its materiality. If the accommodation costs were small relative to other costs that were being assigned throughout the model, then a broad calculation of the average costs for an area would suffice without incurring large distortions in the model. However, where there are real material differences in the type of buildings that are used by different departments, then care must be taken to account for this in the model. A pharmaceutical company may have a high-tech research facility, a processing factory, office blocks and warehouses. All of these will have quite different costs per square metre.

A weighting could be used to reflect the degree to which the average area costs should be assigned to each department. A more detailed ledger may already have the actual costs shown for each building or occupying department.

A building can be made into a cost pool by bringing together such things as rent and rates, utilities, cleaning contracts, maintenance costs and so forth. The cost pool would be assigned to the occupying sections on an area or headcount basis, and then assigned to activities. The key to breaking down the ledger costs is to know how the resources and department data are to be used at the level of activity analysis. The categorization of costs can be at function, department, section or activity level, as shown in Figure 7.3. For example:

1. Marketing costs could be treated as a total, as these could be considered as sustaining costs and would not be analysed at the activity level. However, Marketing expenditure may be in two parts – the sustaining element of brand advertising, and a specific promotion assigned to the product being promoted.
2. Personnel costs can be treated as a total, as these could be the internal service costs and would be reassigned to all other departments on, say, the basis of each department's headcount.
3. Finance costs could be broken down into:
   – 'invoicing', which would be a frontline customer-related cost to be analysed at the activity level

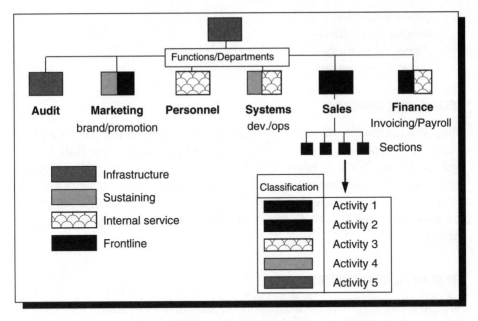

**Figure 7.3**  Categorizing costs

- 'payroll', which would be an internal service cost and would be reassigned to other departments based on, say, headcount
- both Sales and Operations costs, which would be broken down into more departments with some detailed sub-expenditure headings, and then analysed at the activity level
- 'Audit & Legal', which would be treated as a total, as this function would be an infrastructure cost and would not be analysed at the activity level.

For a detailed analysis, the attributes of cost type can be used at the activity level. In this case, some activities in a frontline section, such as Sales, could have a sustaining activity such as 'contribute to five-year planning forecasts'. In the model, the sustaining activities would be assigned to a sustaining cost object such as 'five-year planning costs' which would collect activity costs from all sources that have something to do with this topic.

## UNDERSTANDING COST DRIVERS

The key to assigning costs throughout an ABM model is the use of resource and activity drivers. It is useful to think of cost drivers under four categories:

1. volume cost drivers
2. structural cost drivers
3. change cost drivers
4. introduction cost drivers.

## VOLUME COST DRIVERS

These are the familiar drivers of activity, and are expressed in basic throughput terms. The activities could be driven by weight (tonnes of coal shovelled), volume (gallons of beer bottled), labour hours (machining aluminium castings), claims paid (in an insurance company), or loans advanced (by a bank. Activities linked to volume cost drivers are generally known as *direct* activities. This category is known well in manufacturing companies, but can be used equally well in service industries.

## STRUCTURAL COST DRIVERS

Structural cost drivers uncover the segmentation that exists within the business, the root of complexity, and the cause of a high proportion of the costs. They expose the impact of such things as the:

● range of components
● range of suppliers
● range of product types
● types of delivery made
● mix of order types
● range of customers.

If the cost of handling all these variants were subsumed by treating them as being directly linked to volumes of throughput, then the real cause-and-effect relationship would remain hidden.

## CHANGE COST DRIVERS

No organizations remain static for long periods. Change, of various sorts, drives many activities within a business. Two significant examples of change are:

1. the introduction of new products, or services
2. the 'churn' experienced by companies when old customers are 'changed' for new ones.

We will look at the characteristics of these 'change' cost drivers in turn.

   If the standard cost of introducing a new component only considered the 'direct' costs of acquisition, then a significant number of activities remain buried in the general overheads. When a new component is created, the stock management system will need to be updated, the stores will need to allocate additional stock locations, staff may need training to apply a different technique in assembly, quality assurance may need to be upgraded, special testing equipment may have to be leased, and so on. All these additional costs are a consequence of introducing the new component.

### CASE STUDY

At a bus manufacturing company, an ABM exercise revealed the true costs of introducing new parts. The Design department then changed its emphasis, and supporting systems, to ensure that each new range of bus contained as many existing parts as possible. Any new parts designed for a new type of bus had part numbers that included a reference to the new model. Over the years, the bill of materials for the latest bus showed the distribution of part numbers that were retained from models going back over the previous ten years. Surprisingly, although style and comfort appeared to be significantly improved over the years, this still represented only a small change in the variety of parts used. A by-product of this policy appeared in a reduction in the previous proliferation of spares that had to be held or made as specials, with a consequential increase in service levels and profitability of the Spares division.

Externally driven churn arises when the market for a product or service is very competitive and customer loyalty is low. This can be exacerbated when competing companies encourage churn by offering inducements for customers to switch suppliers. The finance sector fell into this trap. The inducements cost money, and the cost of customer churn increased.

### CASE STUDY

A bank had 250 000 mortgage customers. Every year, 50 000 people redeemed their mortgage and 50 000 new customers came on to the books. In an attempt to increase the number of customers, a cash-back low-interest scheme was devised. Although initially successful, competitors soon emulated and bettered the bank's offers. The net result was an increase in customers to 300 000, but with an ongoing churn of 70 000 customers. The additional customers they attracted were the type that had even less loyalty.

81

Internally driven churn, such as staff turnover, could be a factor. People leave companies for many reasons. Each time it happens, a churn cost is created.

## CASE STUDIES

An insurance company had believed that its salesforce turnover of nearly 50 per cent was 'normal' for the industry. The ABM analysis highlighted the real cost of this churn in people, and the impact this had on profitability. The custom-and-practice attitude was quickly replaced with a policy to improve staff retention.

A manufacturing company grew in volume terms, but declined in profitability. The unit costs of production changed little. The impact of the burgeoning overheads depressed profit. The ABM analysis found that a significant churn cost driver was associated with the career development method of moving people from one job to another frequently. The growth in business size was masking the impact of having most management positions filled with people continually on steep learning curves.

## INTRODUCTION COST DRIVERS

Another type of cost is associated with the introduction of something, such as the activities of design and development. These costs would generally be classified as sustaining, but they have a very high leverage on the direct and frontline activities at a later time. Although the introduction costs may be small in relation to the mainstream production costs, the introduction activities determine the level of mainstream costs. Ongoing costs are designed into the product or service. A traditional approach to product or service development was to have a process that passed the work of one department over a 'high wall' into the next department. Multi-discipline parallel development, also involving suppliers, is now commonly found to create right-first-time designs, designed for production, developed in shorter lead times, to arrive at a lower designed-in cost.

## COST DRIVER VARIABILITY

The relationship of a cost driver to the costs it drives is fundamental to ABM. Total costs divided by the volume of the driver provides the cost per unit cost driver. The assumption in this statement is that each occurrence of the driver creates the same amount of cost. In reality, this cannot be true in every case. The question is therefore one of assessing how appropriate the assumption is. If the actual

measured costs of processing every single sale invoice were exactly the same, then there would be no distribution curve to represent the cost profile.

By taking a number of samples of invoices, we might find a flatter distribution, or even two points to the curve. Where the data suggests that the average value may be misleading, then it may be necessary to find a suitable segmentation of the data by having two activities instead of one, and thus two cost drivers. In the case of sales invoices, this may be due to the different processes involved in dealing with two quite different types of customer.

The scale of the activity has to be taken into account when considering whether to split activities in relation to cost drivers. For example, if a manufacturing company has set-up times that are a significant proportion of total machining time, then set-up time has to be considered separately. This would be a cost driver that reflected the frequency with which set-ups were required. However, set-ups may be component- or product-specific in the sense that the variability depends on the sequence in which batches are run.

## CASE STUDY

A steel tube manufacturer changed its sales policy to tap into a niche market that made to order on short lead times. In the past, it had produced large batches of different types of tube which it made in a preferred sequence, reflecting optimum set-up times at each manufacturing stage. Once the sequence of orders started to dominate the sequence of set-ups, the impact on set-up times became apparent. In the Heat Treatment department, the preferred sequence of steels meant that the first batch was at a low temperature, followed by those that needed incrementally increasing temperatures. It was quicker to heat up a furnace to get to the next batch temperature than it was to let heat dissipate to arrive at a reduced temperature. The niche market therefore came at a cost that had to be accounted for in order to maintain profitability.

When should you take account of variability? The issue is again one of materiality. The balance is between complexity in the model and the credibility of the results from the model. For the model to be useful, and accepted by management as a decision-making tool, any variability of key cost drivers should be included. This usually results in activities being split down into smaller ones, and separate cost drivers being found for each smaller activity.

## ACTIVITY DATA

The key factor to consider when collecting data is the purpose to which the ABM model is to be put. Data can be collected at various levels of detail, as shown in Figure 7.4:

- Level 1 – costs grouped together for high-level reporting, such as by function or process
- Level 2 – costs in the ABM model, where activities are at a level where one cost driver is linked to a particular activity
- Level 3 – a level of detail whereby the type of activity can be examined with a view to improving a process.

For both Levels 2 and 3, it is essential that the data be collected through face-to-face dialogue with the people doing the work. The data is then not only a truer reflection of what is actually happening, but it also creates ownership of the decisions resulting from the analysis of the data in the ABM model.

During the planning stage of building the model, care should be taken to determine which functions, departments or sections will have which level of activity detail. Clearly, every section in an organization can detail all its activities. However, in an internal service department, such as Training, it may only be necessary to have an activity at Level 1. However, if the Head of Training is particularly interested in knowing the unit cost of one of the activities, such as 'setting up

| Level 1<br>Summary level | Level 2<br>Cost model | Level 3<br>Process improvement |
|---|---|---|
| (Process) | (Activities linked to drivers) | (Understanding the types of activities to improve processes) |
| Key customer management | Customer maintenance | Administration<br>Travelling<br>Problem-solving<br>Analysis<br>Reporting |
| | Prospecting for new customers | Research<br>Planning<br>Travelling<br>Meetings<br>Quotations |

**Figure 7.4**   Levels of detail to collect activity data

a course', then more detailed activity and cost driver data can be collected in a later development of the model.

The risk with all model-building is that it feels safer to collect detail on everything, on the basis of not wanting to miss anything. ABM models are very flexible. If more detail would provide more valuable information, then it can be collected at a later date. Starting by being buried in data can mean that no results ever appear.

## ASSIGNING COSTS FROM THE LEDGER TO ACTIVITIES

Costs in the ledger shown by department have to be assigned to the activities in that department. Taking a simplified example, salaries featured on the ledger of a company as actuals for each department. Rent and rates were simply assigned to each department on the ledger on the basis of the area occupied by the department. The business only occupied one building. The next step was to decide the basis on which costs were to be assigned to the activities in the department. For the cost elements of salaries and rent and rates for the call-centre, the resource driver was determined to be headcount. Percentage of time on each activity is the equivalent of headcount.

Through interviews with supervisors and staff in the call-centre, the activities and percentages of time were found to be as shown in Figure 7.5.

Applying the resource driver volumes (percentage of time) to the cost elements enabled the costs for each activity to be calculated in the model.

Once all the activities were in the database, each activity was given a process 'attribute'. Activities in all the other departments in the same process were given the same attribute so that they could be brought together from the database. The activity 'C3 Telephone reads' is part of the 'collections process'. Other activities from different departments featured the same 'collections process' attribute, such as 'read meters' in Field Services and 'bank money' in the Cashiers Department.

| Activity | Description | Use of time |
|---|---|---|
| C1 Perform changes of tenancy | Change of tenancy details | 25% |
| C2 Complaints | Handle customer complaints | 10% |
| C3 Telephone reads | Customer phones in meter reading | 55% |
| C4 Queries | Customer disagrees with bill | 10% |

**Figure 7.5** Activity and time data

When building an ABM model, the planning stage is used to determine how costs on the ledger will be assigned to functions, departments, sections and activities.

## REASSIGNING INTERNAL SERVICE DEPARTMENT COSTS TO OTHER DEPARTMENTS

In the example above, the call-centre was a frontline department. For an internal service department such as Training, the costs from the ledger would only be assigned to the department, and not onwards to its own activities, as the whole of Training would be reassigned to other departments which receive training. The model had already assigned ledger costs to the Training department. These costs were reassigned to other departments on the basis of the 'headcount' in other departments that received training. The training costs for a department were then further reassigned to the activities in that department on the basis of the percentage of time on each activity.

So far in this example, the methods to assign general ledger costs (the cost elements) to the activities have been straightforward. However, in most cases concerns about the assignment methods start to arise for many reasons to do with the complexities in the organization. Some examples of complexity are illustrated below.

Managers' and supervisors' costs may not be included in the total staff costs for a department. In this case, if the managers' and supervisors' costs were a separate line on the ledger at departmental level, then they can be treated as an internal service cost and are reassigned over the frontline activities on the basis of percentage of time that staff spend on the activities.

We may only have total staff costs, but members of staff who are paid a considerably different amount to people working on the majority of activities could perform a specialist activity in the department. For example, the more highly skilled staff who handle 'queries' might be paid twice as much as colleagues in the same department. In this case we can use weighting to calculate the equivalent number of normal staff that the 'query' staff represent. The new headcount equivalent percentage is then used to calculate any costs being assigned using the headcount resource driver.

Sometimes we will find that an activity should be reassigned to other activities to better reflect the influence of certain cost drivers. In this electricity supply company example, the Meter Reading department had listed 'travel' as a separate activity. After discussions with staff, it made more sense to reassign the travel to the reasons for travel, namely the activities of 'read meters (normal)' and 'read meters (emergency)'. The proportions of travel associated with the two other activities were found and used to reassign the travel activity cost. The key cost drivers were then those that applied to the meter-reading activities (number of customers requiring each type of service), rather than the number of miles travelled in total.

Certain costs, such as sub-contracted work for a particular customer, are assigned directly to the final cost object (the customer), as there are no internal activities to allocate the cost to. This is similar to the way that direct materials are assigned to particular products.

Each organization building an ABM model will find that many questions arise as the model progresses. There are few standard answers. However, you must always come back to the same overarching questions: 'What business issues is the model trying to address?', 'Is the cost in question material to the outputs from the model?', and 'Has a reasonable balance been struck between credibility of the model and the model's complexity?'

Whenever a discussion concerning the options of how to treat a cost has reached a conclusion, the ABM team should employ constant diligence and discipline in writing down the arguments and final assumptions that are being used in the model. At a later date, when an argument for using a different option is found to be superior, then this should also be written up when the model construction is changed. One's own memory should not be trusted, even for a day. Also, when the model is periodically refreshed and updated, it is virtually impossible to trace all the assumptions built into it purely by extrapolating from all the links between resources, activities and cost objects.

## REASSIGNING IT DEPARTMENT COSTS TO OTHER DEPARTMENTS

Assigning the IT department's costs is a multi-stage process, to ensure simplicity and clarity in the model. The IT department would have great difficulty trying to find out how much of their Operations section's costs should be assigned to activities in other parts of the business. There are no obvious cost drivers that link the two. Similarly, departments using IT would have difficulty trying to assess what proportion of a computer network's costs should be assigned to their activities. The multi-stage process is shown in Figure 7.6.

The definable entities that link the IT department to the users of IT are the current systems being used. The first stage assigns the costs in the IT department to the systems. For example, the Operations section's costs could be assigned to the hardware using the cost driver of the proportion of time spent in running the various types of hardware being used. The hardware costs (lease or depreciation) plus the Operations costs could be assigned to each system based on the proportion of time each piece of hardware is used to run the systems.

From the user's perspective, the activities using various systems are easy to identify. The system costs are then assigned to activities based on the activity

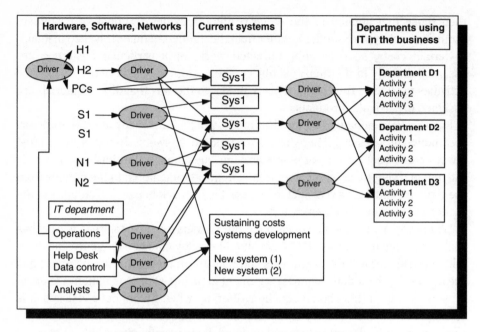

**Figure 7.6**    The multi-stage process to assign IT costs

times (or percentage of time, or headcount). In most cases, this approach passes the test of materiality. Other approaches may claim greater accuracy but introduce greater complexity, and make the model difficult to refresh and update.

Within the IT department there will be a level of systems development taking place. These costs are in the category of sustaining: they are an investment to secure a return in the future. Such costs are not assigned to current systems, and therefore do not pass on to activities in the user departments. As well as the costs of the analysts and programmers working on developments, parts of the hardware, software and network costs would also be assigned to the sustaining category. Reporting the sustaining costs by each system being developed helps IT management track costs and benefits once a new system is introduced.

## PRODUCT AND CUSTOMER PROFITABILITY

The next step to complete a model is to assign the frontline activities to the cost objects: the products, channels and customers. Activity drivers and their volumes have to be found that relate activities to the cost objects. For products, there will be direct costs associated with the people costs where the cost driver would be, say, 'machining hours'. Other direct costs would be raw material, say, 'tonnes used', or the actual cost of bought-out parts. Indirect costs like inspection or machine setting would have cost drivers based on, say, 'batches loaded'. Further away from direct manufacture, other overhead activities such as materials handling require cost drivers that reflect the way the work is being done and how that work is associated with each product.

In the service sector, the nature of the product may be harder to define. A product could be 'bank loans' or broken down into types of loan. For an insurance company, the product could be defined as all the costs and activities to set up a particular type of new policy on the system. Subsequent activities and processes to do with handling the customers' changes of address and other servicing costs could be analysed more effectively through a customer dimension, although such costs could also be brought within the product. The cost of claims on insurance policies would be interesting to analyse both as a product cost and a customer cost. The key is to decide on the issues to be analysed by the model during the planning stage, and then to construct the model with the least complexity to provide the answers.

For the electricity company we are using as an example in this chapter, the notion of 'product' was unusual. The product of electricity was associated with the tariff structure, and related more to the costs of buying electricity from the generators. The key product splits were between the tariff structures for business customers and domestic customers. Within the category of domestic, the key split was between the standard domestic tariff and the economy tariffs for customers receiving a reduced rate for night-time use through a special meter. Certain customer costs could be seen in the context of products, such as fitting special meters. However, the overhead costs in the business that directly related to products, such as the cost of the buyers, were very low in relation to the majority of costs that were associated with customers.

Customer profitability is generally the least understood within companies, as the costs of dealing with customers, other than the Sales department, are largely lost within the normal accounts. Even where the Sales department's costs are clearly known, allocating them on the basis of the sales value taken by each customer would lead to highly erroneous calculations of profitability.

In the ABM model, the products (or services) that the customer is buying are assigned to customers, as well as the costs and activities to service the customers. If, for example, the customers fell into three segments, X, Y and Z, then for the activity of 'visit customers' the activity driver of 'visits' needs the total volume of visits split between the three segments. The proportions of activity driver volumes determine how much of the activity cost is to be assigned to each of the cost objects.

Driver volumes are generally found from transaction files that already exist in the organization. For example, the salesforce's log sheets of how they used their time, or the Sales ledger for number of customers by type. Where the data does not exist, then a first approximation would be someone's best guess, though it is always prudent to start some level of data recording for a representative period in order to have credible figures.

But what determines the customer segments to use as cost objects? Any parameters that are known about the customers can be used to create segments. The issue for each organization undertaking ABM is to decide what will be the relevance of the data coming from the model, and how would it be used to improve processes and customer mix. At the highest level, the segment could just be 'all customers'. In our example company, the two major segments of business customers and domestic customers was a first split. Within domestic, they could be further split by geographic location, those in the North and South, or further down to individual postcode district. The segmentation could be by the type of process they initiate in the business, such as the method used to pay bills, or it could be by the customers' behaviours, such as those that pay bills on time and those that don't.

For the electricity company, a key issue to resolve concerned finding out which customers were profitable or unprofitable and why, then using this data to create an acquisition and retention strategy for profitable customers and not waste money on unprofitable customers. The latter segment could drift to competitors. However, certain unprofitable segments were likely to remain as customers, so the extra processes they initiated had to become highly efficient. The ABM model thus had to provide the profitability of every single customer, and then by using a range of attributes for each customer, aggregate them into meaningful segments based on the sub-process they created in the business.

A segment could be 'all customers who pay by direct debit'. Another could be 'all customers that only pay when a final demand is issued'. For each customer so defined, the ABM model provided all the costed activities that could be set against the revenue to determine customer profitability.

## USING UNIT COSTS FOR ANALYSIS

Unit costs, the total activity cost divided by the driver volume, are a powerful means of displaying the data. The costs of all the activities that could occur in the 'bill creation' process, best and worst case, are shown in Figure 7.7.

Clearly, any customer that incurs the whole sequence of activities is very expensive to the business. The requirement is to uncover the population of customers that incur the various mixes of activities, and then propose ways of changing the mix of customers or reduce the unit costs. In a typical core process such as billing, unwanted activities occurred either created by certain customers (they failed to pay on time) or by internal process failures (posting payments to wrong accounts). To make all the processes, unit costs and driver volumes visible, an event chart can be drawn to display the ABM data. A simplified version of the 'collections' process is shown in Figure 7.8.

| Meter-reading activities | Unit cost | Cumulative process costs | |
| --- | --- | --- | --- |
| | | Ideal | Worst case |
| Access on first visit | 0.51 | 0.51 | |
| No access on first visit | 0.46 | | 0.46 |
| Access on second visit | 1.98 | | |
| No access on second visit | 1.65 | | 1.38 |
| Appointment | 14.78 | | 16.16 |
| (evening or Saturday) | 2.01 | | 18.17 |
| Compiling warrant, swearing in court | 12.11 | | 30.28 |
| First warrant visit | 24.67 | | 54.95 |
| Second warrant visit | 24.67 | | 79.62 |
| Bill prepared and posted to customer | 0.28 | 0.79 | 79.90 |

**Figure 7.7**   Cumulative costs: best and worst case

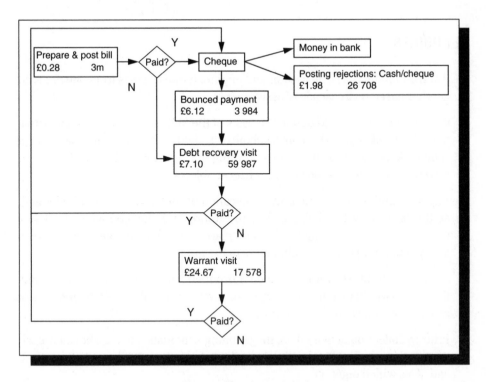

**Figure 7.8**   An event chart

Management now had a simple means to formulate plans to address the issue of segments of customers that created unwanted costs in the business. The event chart can be used to track the impact of changing the customer mix over periods of time. Where there were significant process failures, actions could be put in place and the impact on unit and total costs tracked over time. To initiate process improvements, event charts were used to bring together representatives from the various departments that featured in the overall process.

Unit cost data also provided a means to benchmark parts of the process, either internally by comparing various geographic regions, or externally with comparable organizations or published best-practice data. The unit cost data formed the basis for Activity Based Budgeting. By predicting a number of scenarios concerning customer attrition by customer segment as well as customer gain by segment, the new mix of customers could be fed back into the model and the new level of activities and then resources calculated. The power of the ABM data is that any number of 'What if?' scenarios can be modelled quickly and related to other initiatives such as specific marketing campaigns with their associated costs. The predicted outcome and the actual outcome of a specific promotion can be monitored, and the results used to refine the next campaign.

## KEY POINTS

- An ABM model is a large assignment engine. It moves costs from one entity to another based on a cascade of assignments.

- Cost drivers are used to define the basis of the logic to assign costs and activities. When planning the construction of a model, it is wise to start with a schematic version drawn on paper showing the logic that will be used to assign resources to activities and activities to cost objects.

- Any assumptions concerning the application of the drivers should be logged, as the basis may be challenged in the future and changed as a result (for example, start with average costs per square metre, but change to actual costs for each building as a later refinement of the model).

- Activities can be shown in the model grouped within departments and functions. This would match the organizational structure and current boundaries of cost centres shown in the accounts.

- Prior to collecting activity data, the planning schematic should show, for each department, the level of detail to be collected, whether attributes will be used, and, if so, which ones.

- An important consideration at the planning stage is to define the sources of activity driver data. Much of the data will come from the company's current transaction files, but other data may be non-existent. Knowing this at the planning stage allows more time for data creation in the areas where the driver volumes and proportions by cost object will be assigning significant costs through the model.

- A key issue when determining how to handle each type of cost in the ledger is its materiality. Agonizing over how to assign a cost that is 0.01 per cent of the total is not material to the outcome from the model.

- *Volume cost drivers* are expressed in basic throughput terms: for example, litres bottled, invoices processed.

- *Structural cost drivers* uncover the segmentation that exists within the business: for example, range of components, suppliers, product types.

- *Change cost drivers* uncover how changes to the status quo have an impact on the business: for example, new product introduction, customer churn.

- *Introduction cost drivers* relate to the activities to do with the future: for example, design and development.

- *Cost driver variability* tests how strong a suspected *pro rata* relationship exists between an activity and the chosen driver. Variability exists if it is found that more than one driver is acting on the activity. This usually results in activities being split down into smaller ones, and separate cost drivers being found for each smaller activity.

- Unit costs, the total activity cost divided by the driver volume, are a powerful means of displaying the data. Unit cost data also provides a means to benchmark parts of the process, either internally by comparing various geographic regions, or externally with comparable organizations or published best-practice data. Unit cost data forms the basis for Activity Based Budgeting.

# 8 Undertaking an ABM project

## OBJECTIVES OF THE PROJECT

Embarking on an ABM project is not a trivial exercise. Like any project that has to make a significant impact on business performance, it will require dedicated resources, the co-operation of the business in becoming involved in the task of data collection, and the determination of the top team to use the results to improve the organization's fortunes.

If an ABM project starts as a sole initiative from the Finance function, promoted as a new means of costing, then the project will have a poor chance of success. The success of ABM comes from every function seeing uses for the model outputs, both from a functional perspective and from a process perspective for the business as a whole. The top team collectively should all be very interested in making product and customer profitability visible. Further, the outputs from the model need to be seen by everyone as the fundamental base of knowledge enabling them to make better decisions on the products or services portfolio, the mix of customers the company wishes to acquire and nurture, and serving as the launch pad for significant process improvement.

Also, beware the 'ABM evangelists' surrounded by an auroral glow fresh from an ABM conference expounding loudly on the elegance of the analysis embodied in an ABM model. The end result may well be a model that is a benchmark in its own right. However, without a real business purpose for creating it, such a model will languish in a cupboard next to many other laudable projects that started with high hopes but ended without any measurable outcomes.

If the primary aim were profitability analysis, then the initial model would generally start with activity analysis at a high level. However, if, as we saw with the electricity company example, the customer segmentation is determined by the myriad detailed processes created by customers, then the activity analysis is necessarily far more detailed.

If the aim of the model is to establish profitability first, followed by process improvement, then activity data needs to be detailed enough to pick up the failure activities, and through attributes prepared in a way that readily allows process analysis by type of activity.

During any ABM project, it is invariably the case that as the model starts to deliver new and significant insights about the business, this prompts further questions. Not all such questions can be determined at the outset during the planning stage. In these situations, the flexibility of ABM comes to the fore. At any stage, more detailed data collection can supplement any initial high-level data. At any stage, where the model is deemed to be particularly sensitive to a range of cost drivers rather than the initial raw driver chosen, the activities and drivers can be modified. At any stage, if subtle insights can be obtained by further segmenting the customer categories, appropriate activity drivers can be found to assign activities to a more detailed level. The only discipline that must be followed rigidly is to keep the log of changes to the model completely up to date.

## KEY STEPS

The ABM process steps outlined here are generic. Care needs to be taken to ensure that for each ABM project, the specific steps to follow and the detailed content of each step are tailored to the needs of the company. Table 8.1 consists of a checklist of each step (left-hand column) and the desired outcome (right-hand column), and is a useful guideline for most ABM projects.

**Table 8.1    ABM process checklist**

*Project start-up and detailed planning*

| | |
|---|---|
| Establish Steering Group and Project Team | Project properly resourced and managed |
| Confirm objectives | Expectations agreed |
| Provide thorough pre-project training in the principles and practice of ABM techniques | Role of the team and ABM understood by the team |
| Prepare and undertake briefing/communications to senior managers | Awareness of project, its aims, degree of staff involvement |
| Define products, channels and customers to be costed | Scope of the analysis determined |
| Assess characteristics of segmentation and availability of sources of data | Boundary of accuracy of analysis determined |
| Preliminary identification of processes, activities and drivers | Provisional list (or map) of processes |
| Assess suitability of general ledgers for analysis and agree period | Areas of risk identified and agreed with Steering Group |
| Select systems to capture and model activity-based data | Systems requirement agreed and actioned (and software acquired) |
| Detailed work step planning | Steering Group signs off plan |

*Continued*

*Established preliminary understanding of cost dynamics*

| | |
|---|---|
| In key areas, such as Sales, Customer Service, Production, etc., make field visits to understand the business | Project informed by a deep understanding of the work and the customer-facing issues |
| Outline process maps created | 'Helicopter' view of the business seen by team |

*Activity and cost driver identification and activity quantification*

| | |
|---|---|
| Review organization, processes, activities and cost drivers with managers | Dictionary of activities and cost drivers confirmed |
| Identify sources of quantitative data for activities, cost drivers and cost driver variability | Sources identified (such as current recorded data, need for interview, etc.) |
| Capture time allocations to activities | Basic data found |
| Agree assignment of non-staff costs and other non-frontline costs | Provisional costing model in paper schematic form |

*Development of activity costs and their validation by managers*

| | |
|---|---|
| Agree basis of assigning of general ledger costs to activities (resource drivers) | Resources to activities links established |
| Classify activities by type and by process | Basis for further analysis created |
| Build first-stage ABM model to reflect cost assignments and activity type, and reconcile activity costs to general ledger | Foundation of ABM model built |
| Review activity costs with managers | Buy-in by management to activity costs |

*Cost driver volumes*

| | |
|---|---|
| Identify suitable sources of cost driver data for a suitable period and any surrogate drivers where necessary | Refined cost driver dictionary |
| Download or manually record as appropriate | Basis for calculating activity cost per unit cost driver (output costing) |
| Review with managers and compare volume variations with level of driven activities | Management confidence in selection of cost drivers |
| Where material, record cost driver variability | An understanding of where to apply greater sensitivity to the ABM model |

*Revenue data*

| | |
|---|---|
| Capture revenue by product, channel, customer, and any other segment of interest | Basis for product, channel and customer profitability |
| Download hard data via Management Information System, or input manually | Model loaded |
| Review revenue data with managers | Buy-in by managers |

*Continued*

97

---

*Model-building and validation*

---

| | |
|---|---|
| Design final structure of model, and agree principles with Steering Group | Key principles agreed |
| Build second stage of model, and apply cost driver and revenue data | Model structure resident on PC |
| Reconcile to general ledgers | Logic check complete |
| Review activity costs and output costs with department managers, and amend model as necessary | Buy-in by managers |

---

*Analysis and interpretation of ABM model output*

---

| | |
|---|---|
| Analysis by activity costs by activity, cost driver, process, product, channel and customer segments | Insights into the activity structure of the business, its processes and cost drivers |
| Analysis of product, channel and customer profitability | Understanding of areas of profit erosion and profit opportunity |
| Feedback to management of all analyses | Buy-in by managers |
| Development, with management, of changing strategies (discounts, margins, segments, etc.) to improve profitability | Comparison of 'What-if?' scenarios |
| Development, with managers, of better processes to improve profitability | Focus for management action |

---

*Review of output from project and agreement of next steps*

---

| | |
|---|---|
| Presentation to Steering Group and senior management of the complete model, its structure, and the bases on which it has been developed (assumptions and data capture period) | Ownership of the ABM model by the Board, and recognition of the importance of model as a tool to assist effective decision-making within the business |
| Presentation of significant findings, conclusions and recommendations, and discussion of the options available to improve overall profitability | Management action plans that respond to the ABM information generated by the project (customer retention, divestment and acquisition strategies, process re-engineering, pricing policies, service levels, etc.) |

---

*Concluded*

# AREAS OF POTENTIAL DIFFICULTY

All projects have difficulties. In ABM, these are mainly concerned with data, and the resources available to search for and supply it. Some of the difficulties you might encounter include addressing:

- the ease with which data will be available to segment the customer base
- the extent to which data contained within the general ledgers is appropriately structured to support product, channel and customer profitability analysis

- the extent to which it will be sensible to identify and quantify activities in a sample of the organization and then extrapolate these to the whole of the organization; this is particularly relevant where, say, a multi-regional structure appears to be consistent across the whole country
- the ease with which data can be extrapolated via current systems, and the degree to which this is up to date and accurate
- the ease with which data concerning cost drivers is available from existing records and checking that it is appropriate
- ensuring that the staff needed to provide data on data collection forms, via interviews or workshops, are available and knowledgeable
- making a project team available for the duration of the ABM project, preferably on a full-time basis; they should also have the aptitude and skills to undertake the work; a core team is required for the duration of the project and will have responsibility for building the actual ABM model; members of the core team will become a 'centre of excellence' for ABM, once the main project has concluded its work; the core team may be extended into a larger team by including additional full- or part-time members for the stages that involve data collection.

## SOFTWARE

ABM models can be built on spreadsheets, but only the most basic type of analysis can be undertaken in this way. The creation of spreadsheets to handle the assignments of resources and activities soon spawns vast complex look-up tables and multiple sheets, growing organically as the demands for more analysis are built in. The main disadvantage of spreadsheets is that they are rarely documented as they are built. Only the creator can remember – and then only vaguely – how it was all put together.

Database tools offer a lot of the functionality required to undertake ABM analysis, but on their own are still unable to meet all the necessary requirements of a model.

The best fit is obtained from using proprietary ABM software. Packages are available which are robust and easy to use and have been subjected to continuous development over at least ten years. Such software has been designed to facilitate the building of large models of high complexity, while at the same time making it easy to track the logic of the cost assignments. The software includes simple links to import and export data from and to other spreadsheet and database tools, as well as packages to present the output from analyses in graphical format. The key is to obtain powerful ABM software, managed by the ABM experts, with straightforward, easy to assimilate outputs fed to any number of managers' desks where decisions are taken.

An ABM model requires fast processing power, but sufficient power is available on most modern desktop PCs. In a team environment, each member can work on building parts of the model and entering activity and driver data on their own machine, periodically integrating the data into the main model via the team's network. The team should also have access to the company's transaction files.

Depending on the size of the business and the level of integration required in the longer term, the ABM model can be linked on a more permanent basis to the company's main systems and files. This may involve feeding from the normal transaction files, or from and to a data warehouse. For geographically dispersed businesses, data feeds via the Internet can also be established. Proprietary ABM software keeps abreast of modern integration requirements.

## TEAM RESOURCES

An ABM team should represent all the main functions within the business, rather than being a team of financial specialists drawn from the Finance function. The team needs to bring knowledge of the business into the project at the start, to ensure that the data collection and analysis planning stage creates a series of project steps that will provide outputs that answer the key questions raised by the business.

Team members need to be credible individuals. They will be interacting with the rest of the business at all levels: gathering data, analysing outputs, drawing conclusions and making recommendations to the senior team. Once the ABM project is completed, the model becomes a dynamic decision support tool. Most team members will return to the business, while a nucleus will continue to keep the model up to date and work with managers to extract the maximum value from the model. When ABM is part of 'business as usual', then ABM can be termed a success.

## USE OF CONSULTANTS

The use of consultants to support an ABM project would follow the usual criteria for seeking outside help. ABM consultants provide expert knowledge of the selection of appropriate software, and they will have undertaken many similar projects. Their key role is to help steer the company during the planning and model-building stages, to speed implementation, and to avoid pitfalls.

Consultants should transfer skills and knowledge to the client team and build a centre of expertise among the company's team members. Further, they should assist the process of embedding ABM in the company, both technically and by ensuring that ABM becomes a tool which provides daily support to managers. When using consultants, it is important not to put them in the position of building the model without any client team involvement at all. This is a recipe for creating a perfect model that nobody ever uses.

## EMBEDDING AND REFRESHING

Key measures of success of an ABM project are:

- the credibility and ownership that the inputs and results of the ABM model achieve among middle and senior management
- the speed with which the project can be used to influence decision-making
- the degree to which the project creates a self-sustaining centre of ABM expertise in the organization capable of maintaining the use of ABM on an ongoing basis
- the extent to which ABM implementation brings significant benefits to the business.

An important aspect of the ABM project is the technical embedding of the methods employed so that future refreshes of data can be achieved quickly and with fewer resources. During the ABM project phase, data collection, particularly the collection of cost driver volumes, usually involves analysing a wide range of company systems' files from a number of sources. These analyses are normally completed 'offline' within the team. Where possible, these analyses need to be automated so that the relevant data to refresh and update the model can be downloaded from the company's systems with little need for manual manipulation.

The initial model-building is based on a number of assumptions concerning level of detail, relevance of certain cost types, and so on. The initial approach tends to err on the side of caution, in that too much detail finds its way into the model. During the project, the team will have analysed the business in some depth and will be able to stand back to make a judgement on data relevance once the model has been created. With the knowledge gained during the model-building, and in conjunction with business managers, the team will be in a position to simplify the model in areas where such a change does not materially affect the outputs from the model. For example, there may be too many activities in a department, each costing very little. If carried out in partnership with business managers, the ownership of each part of the model will remain with line management.

The results from the first ABM model represent a snapshot of the organization. Although there will be great interest in the output, it will not be long before the results will diminish in impact because they are perceived to be dated. The model will need to be refreshed so that it is up to date – a dynamic reflection of the current reality. The model has to remain credible if managers are to base critical decisions on the outputs.

A refresh of the model typically needs to capture the following:

- actual costs or forecasts that are recent
- the latest driver quantities
- changes to the most significant activities in the model, particularly if process re-engineering has already started.

In addition to providing new information to the organization, a refresh will help to speed the embedding process and increase the ability of the ABM team to maintain the use of ABM for the foreseeable future.

## USING ABM OUTPUTS FOR PERFORMANCE IMPROVEMENT

ABM model outputs provide the basis for performance improvement by business managers. In order to make this work and fuel the demand for ABM to be used:

- business managers, team leaders and supervisors should be provided with information highly relevant to their needs
- the users must be able to apply ABM information and to demand information from the ABM team
- the users must have an understanding of how their own function interacts with others, and how to use ABM information as the catalyst and vehicle to hold meaningful dialogues focused on improvements to unit costs and customer service
- the ABM team and both process change managers and Information System department teams need to work together with complementary skills and appropriate frameworks.

In order to drive the supply of information to meet the demand:

- the ABM team has to be capable of refreshing the model at appropriate frequencies, as governed by regular reviews of what within the model is relevant
- the collection of all data will have to be automated as far as possible
- business managers and others must be willing to collect certain data on an ongoing basis
- a close relationship should be developed between the ABM team and other groups who support change and record the effects, such as process change managers.

An ABM team is ideally placed to help users of ABM data to understand how the different functions interact and therefore allow meaningful dialogue across functions focused on improving unit costs and customer service. The first task is to structure the data into a highly visible and usable form based on the notion of event triggers and cascades of activities. Here are the key stages:

1. The team brainstorms key events (both business and customer-related), and constructs the activity cascades (processes) for the core process and all the branches off it that represent failures, either internal or customer-induced.
2. The team structures output data from the model to reflect the different events, the cascade of activities, cost driver volumes, and both total and unit costs.

The team is then in a position to advise business managers of the multi-function activity cascades within the ABM data, and all the interactions and interdependencies. Where business managers believe that there could be several significant cross-functional issues to be resolved, the ABM team embarks upon a more proactive initiative involving the following steps:

1. Facilitate multi-functional groups of managers in identifying key opportunities to influence unit costs, reduce cycle times and/or influence the behaviour of customers.
2. Set up mechanisms to put improvements in place.
3. Facilitate the groups of managers in identifying measures at appropriate points in the activity cascade, and set up reports at appropriate frequencies. These form the basis of a set of Key Performance Indicators.

## USING ABM FOR COMMERCIAL DECISION SUPPORT

Business process management is about improvement: better efficiency and effectiveness. Commercial management is concerned with portfolio, pricing and margin management decisions. These decisions concern:

- the range of products or services the company wishes to offer
- the types of customer it wishes to trade with
- whether to make products in-house, or use sub-contractors.

If we needed to know the impact of reducing the product range, or changing the mix of customers, or deciding to use sub-contractors for some of the work, then it is vital to be able to trace the potential decision through to the activities in the organization. We can only know the costs that are avoided as a result if we can trace the costs. Without this knowledge, portfolio decisions would be based on best estimates of the impact – or worse, failure to recognize the true level of avoidable costs, and thus keeping them.

The ABM analysis provides the means to perform customer engineering, by answering basic questions, such as:

- Which are the least profitable customers, and how can we improve their level of profitability?
- How can we protect the relationship with our most profitable customers?
- How can we redirect the salesforce's efforts away from going for volume towards going for profit?
- Is it more profitable to redirect low-volume customers through wholesalers, rather than servicing them direct?
- Should we have a segmented discount structure based on customer attributes relating to service level needs, rather than on total volume supplied?
- What will be the impact of introducing an e-commerce channel to customers via the Web site?

Product and customer profitability analysis provides the basis on which to determine the product and customer portfolio. Those customers having a negative contribution would immediately draw attention to themselves. If the volumes were low and there was little chance of increasing the contribution, then they might become candidates for elimination. The danger with such customers is that sales volumes to them could increase, further dragging down overall company profitability. Problem customers have healthy volumes but low profitability. These require more detailed study to see whether the mix of products is the cause of the problem. Action on selective product pricing might then make the account much more profitable.

Customers with potential are those where higher-volume sales add significantly to overall company profit. Any action on price and volume has a further positive impact on profit, although care should be taken, as such customers are valuable and it is important to retain them.

For any one customer, a product profitability profile shows whether there are any products that are significantly lowering profitability. Actions to change product prices to the customer are difficult to put in place. A unilateral decision to cut out certain products would be unwise: the customer might then transfer all the profitable products to a competitor.

The key to using ABM profitability data is not to take instant action to eliminate any negative products or customers, but to conduct a measured review of the whole relationship with customers. There could well be a strategic reason for continuing in some unprofitable relationships. This may be a short-term position while a market presence is being built up, or it may be to keep competitors out of a segment in one area where the products and customers are profitable in all other areas. The power of using ABM outputs is that managers know the consequences of making decisions, rather than having to wait for an indeterminate result to appear when it is too late to redress a poor decision.

## KEY POINTS

- Embarking on an ABM project is not a trivial exercise.

- Without a real business purpose, an ABM model will languish in a cupboard next to many other laudable projects that started with high hopes but ended without any measurable outcomes.

- At the start of a project, care should be taken to ensure that the specific steps to follow and the detailed content of each step are tailored to the needs of the company.

- All projects have a degree of risk. In ABM, these are mainly concerned with data, and the resources available to search for and supply it.

- Proprietary ABM software is available, which is robust and easy to use and has been subjected to continuous development over at least ten years.

- The ABM project team should have knowledge of the business, to ensure that the data collection and analysis planning stage creates a series of project steps that will provide outputs that answer the key questions raised by the business.

- Team members need to be credible individuals. They will be interacting with the rest of the business at all levels – gathering data, analysing outputs, drawing conclusions, and making recommendations to the senior team.

- ABM consultants provide expert knowledge of the selection of appropriate software, and should have undertaken many similar projects. Their key role is to help steer the company during the planning and model-building stages, to speed implementation, and to avoid pitfalls.

- An important aspect of the ABM project is the technical embedding of the methods employed so that future refreshes of data can be achieved quickly and with fewer resources.

- ABM model outputs provide the basis for performance improvement by business managers.

- ABM model outputs support commercial management in making decisions concerning product portfolio, pricing and margin management, as well as decisions concerning the types of customer it wishes to trade with.

# 9 Integrating improvement approaches

In business, it is difficult to avoid being assailed by three-letter acronyms spelling out the latest approach to improve organizational effectiveness and bring the promise of financial success within the Chief Executive's grasp. But why is it that many promises seem empty and success forever recedes over the next horizon?

Can one tool kit ever solve a business's problems, even assuming that the most appropriate tool kit was chosen in the first place? Patently it cannot, but we still look for the Phoenix of the next solution rising from the ashes of the last failed initiative. For ABM to be a success, it must be seen and used in a broader context, one that provides room for other tools from other tool kits to be integrated into the overall approach. Enabling this to happen means blurring the boundaries that the purists will build around the theory and practice of ABM, or whatever other approach is being used.

## ABM AND BUSINESS PROCESS RE-ENGINEERING

Business Process Re-engineering (BPR) or Business Process Management (BPM) are techniques that replaced the decreasingly popular Total Quality Management (TQM). Where TQM expounded the virtues of going beyond customer needs and involving all employees in applying the tools and techniques of continuous improvement, BPR expounded a more radical approach. For some organizations, it was out with the old and in with the new. If it wasn't radical, then it wasn't re-engineering.

Clearly, there are degrees of everything. At one end of the scale, re-engineering could be considered to be an extension of TQM but with an enhanced cross-functional process perspective. In this case, employees would still be involved in looking at opportunities to make improvements, but with a greater regard for the impact any changes would have on a whole process. At the other end of the scale,

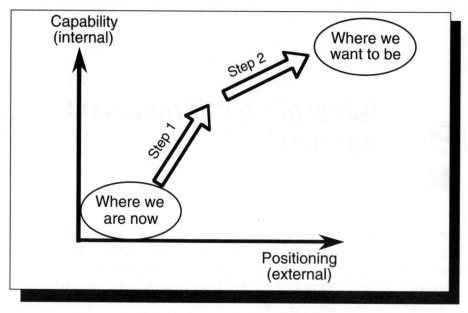

**Figure 9.1** The two steps of the BPR journey

starting with a clean sheet of paper and designing a business from scratch provided an opportunity to be radical and innovative.

Let us look again at the journey of improvement using the map with the axes of *positioning* and *capability*. We now see two steps to the journey, as shown in Figure 9.1.

## PROCESS RE-ENGINEERING: STEP 1

This step in the re-engineering journey looks at current processes in an effort to reduce unit costs and improve customer service to current customers. Step 1 generally starts with a customer needs survey to highlight gaps in the service compared to competitors. This is an action on the *positioning* axis. However, there is a danger that the company will try to enhance services to *all* customers. ABM introduces a vital piece of information at this point by analysing customer profitability. Having selected the segment of customers it wishes to do business with in the future, then only those processes aligned to the selected customers would be re-engineered to enhance the level of service. Without profitability knowledge, providing enhanced services to unprofitable customers runs the risk of attracting even more of them.

On the *capability* axis, a re-engineering initiative would start with collecting data on the activities people undertake, and then use attributes to define the processes and the types of activity that are core to adding value, and those that divert people away from core work because a process has failed. This data provides the basis on which to develop ideas to improve the processes. If activity data is collected with the purpose of re-engineering the processes, it is not too big a leap to assign the activities to the products or services the company provides, and also to the customers the business serves. Product and customer profitability is only a short stride away from a re-engineering project. By the same token, if the activity data for an ABM model included the same attributes, then you are only a short stride away from using the activity data as the basis for re-engineering the processes.

By pausing at the problem-definition stage of an ABM or BPM initiative, the company can have the best of both worlds. Although an integrated approach would take longer than undertaking either one separately, doing them together provides benefits greater than the sum of the individual approaches.

## BUSINESS RE-ENGINEERING: STEP 2

Step 2 takes a different perspective towards the business compared to Step 1. In ABM, costs are categorized into *infrastructure, sustaining, internal service* and *frontline*. Whereas Step 1 concentrates on today's business, improving the effectiveness of the current frontline activities and processes, Step 2 is a vital sustaining activity, in that it takes a longer-term view to design the future business. Step 2 is the key role for the senior team, whose task is to address issues that will take the business to a world-class position with a world class capability. Rather than re-engineering processes, Step 2 re-engineers the business as a whole to deliver a new proposition to the market. As an example of Step 2 and the use of ABM, we will look at a case study in the finance sector, although the logic to build a new proposition works in any type of business.

### CASE STUDY

A traditional insurance company, in common with its competitors, had been through a series of mergers. Although unit costs had reduced through a reduction in the duplicated site locations, managers and staff, nothing had changed in terms of its product and service offerings to customers. Much had been done to improve current processes, but creating clear market differentiation required new thinking.

The first stage of developing a new proposition required an analysis of the key profit drivers in the business. These were:

- *Customer segmentation* – Who were the profitable customers, and what attributes made them profitable? The new business would not offer the proposition to everyone, and it had to be careful only to let the right type of people become customers.
- *Customer retention* – Winning new customers to replace those that went to competitors was a cost that added little value. Retaining customers for life, and knowing how to achieve this, was key to the success of the new business.
- *Purchased components* – Rather than insurance products in the conventional sense, purchased as separate entities, each part of the insurance cover would be a component of the whole proposition. Other components would include giving advice to customers that made them safer and reduced the chances they would need to claim on their insurance policy. From the customers' perspective, this was a service in return for the premiums they paid each month, and decreased the chances of a customer being in a claim situation, an experience people would rather avoid. This helped customer retention, and the company expected to reduce the overall loss ratio, and thus enhance profitability.
- *Unit costs* – By using a one-stop-shop approach to the customer management system and having one policy containing a multitude of insurance covers, process times were significantly reduced. Providing electronic access via the telephone, the Internet and interactive television led to high service levels, fast turn-arounds and low unit costs.
- *Customer-centric organization* – By putting the customer at the heart of the business the need for separate functions and tall hierarchies was eliminated.

The first stage of creating a new proposition was to build a financial model of the new business. The financial model tested the key profit drivers and their sensitivity. Rather than analysing the current business, ABM was used to construct the new business around the key profit drivers. The end of the first stage created a 'Proposition Blueprint'.

The second stage mapped all the customers' life stages, and determined the particular life stages that the proposition was designed to address. This refined the 'components' (products and services) that were to be offered to customers. This stage also started to define the target segment and the criteria that let people become customers. These elements of the design helped refine the original financial model in terms of the income line and the major cost in terms of claims.

Having developed the initial set of components to the selected segment at a specific life stage, the customer contact strategy was then modelled. The mechanism of determining all the 'customer experiences' was used to create the desired differentiation, and thus the expected volume of sales. The end of the second stage created the 'Customer Experience Blueprint'.

The third stage created the operational design of the sales process, other advice-giving processes, links to third-party suppliers of other components, back-office processes, claims processes, and so forth. This stage determined the costs of delivering the proposition, which provided the final refinement of the original ABM financial model. Profit drivers were re-calibrated and the sensitivities re-calculated. Getting profit drivers constantly moving in the right direction was critical to achieving the designed level of profitability.

The end of the third stage was an 'Operational Blueprint' that enabled the proposition to be launched to customers. The original financial model now became the key reporting mechanism to show that the proposition was on track and delivering the expected results.

Building a new business on the foundation of an ABM model is key to retaining a focus on the profit drivers and all the sub-processes that are to be put in place to deliver profit from the right products and services for profitable customers.

## ABM AND VALUE BASED MANAGEMENT

Value Based Management (VBM) is an approach to measuring the performance of a business, setting targets, finding and acting on the key drivers that increase value, and embedding the continuous journey to higher value creation through education and reward mechanisms. The key benefits of VBM are that it:

- unifies the organization by concentrating everyone's efforts on increasing value
- removes dysfunctional behaviours by reducing or eliminating the effect of many traditional measures
- provides management with the analysis and action tools to change those aspects of the business that will increase value
- highlights those aspects of the business that are destroying value, and focuses action on eliminating them.

VBM is a philosophy that puts value-creation at the core of decision-making, a process that links strategy to day-to-day management, and a way of measuring business performance that overcomes the deficiencies of traditional accounting and performance measurement methods. It can be applied to determine how finance capital is to be invested, what work people do, which new products are developed, and what products the business makes and which customers it serves.

VBM is not an exclusive concept: it should be implemented alongside other improvement initiatives, such as re-engineering, continuous improvement and Activity-Based Management, and should complement them.

There are several ways a business can increase its value:

- It can invest in profitable growth by developing new products and markets, or by acquisition.
- It can reduce process costs by re-engineering, continuous improvement, automation, enhancing workflow, and training.
- It can reduce its capital charge by cutting work-in-progress, finished goods stocks and action on debtors and creditors.
- It can identify unprofitable products, customers or businesses, and either find ways to make them profitable, or decide to invest its resources elsewhere.

To maximize value, all the value-driving activities of the company have to be co-ordinated. Projects, decisions, teams, activities, reward mechanisms, performance targets and measures, communications, financial analysis and actions – all need to be focused on the single aim of maximizing value.

The key measure is Shareholder Value Added (SVA), defined as the net operating profit after tax minus the capital charge. The net operating profit after tax brings into focus prices, volumes, the cost of sales and all the operating expenses in the business, as well as taxes. It is therefore imperative that the business knows which products and customers are profitable, and why, using ABM techniques, and that its processes operate at the lowest unit cost, by using BPM techniques.

The capital charge is all capital (net working capital plus net fixed capital) multiplied by the cost of capital. Capital comprises working capital (debtors, creditors and inventory) plus fixed capital (property, plant and equipment). The cost of capital reflects the interest paid on debt and borrowings and the return expected by shareholders (including a premium for the risk involved in taking on equity). In the value calculation, the cost of capital is introduced to ensure that management is confident that it will make more money than the minimum required to pay off loans and satisfy the expectations of shareholders. To reflect the mix of capital used, a Weighted Average Cost of Capital (WACC) needs to be calculated, according to the long-term debt/equity structure the business wishes to achieve.

Increasing value involves identifying those factors in a business that drive value. There are four types of value driver: *revenue, operating, investment* and *finance*. A business can grow its revenue and profit margins by influencing its revenue value drivers:

- *Volume growth* – the mix of products and services, prices, customer loyalty, differentiation and innovation that create the greatest value – ABM provides the underlying information to guide decisions.

- *Market growth* – market share, customer mix and the impact that customers have on the business, both in revenue and cost terms – ABM provides the underlying information to guide decisions.

A business can generate a high cash profit by influencing its operating drivers, ensuring that hard-won revenue is not eroded by the costs of creating revenue:

- *Processes* – the efficiency and effectiveness of activities in all parts of the business
- *Methods* – making the best use of technology, workflow, multi-skilling, out-sourcing, and so on
- *Training* – the costs of enhancing individual and team capability
- *Customers* – the true cost of servicing customers.

A process analysis informed by ABM provides data to understand the operating drivers.

To control cash going out, a company needs to be able to influence its working capital and capital investments:

- *Cash tied up* – inventory and creditors/debtors
- *Cash used* – fixed assets and equipment leasing arrangements
- *Intangible assets* – R&D, intellectual capital, brands, goodwill.

An ABM model designed to create a measure of Shareholder Value Added includes working capital and capital investments.

The business needs to be able to influence the cost of equity and debt that have an impact on its cost of capital:

- *Gearing* – loans and other non-equity financing
- *Risk premiums* – relative stock market position, shareholder expectations and so on, while reducing the level of exposure to tax
- *Cash tax* – transfer pricing and holding company location.

Many businesses have become highly proficient in improving the efficiency and effectiveness of their processes. But there's a limit to how far you can shrink your-self. Investing in growth – new products and services, markets and businesses – deserves equal priority. A failure to match improvement in efficiency with growth invariably leads to gradual loss of competitiveness.

Value Based Management can be applied to identify what value each business unit adds, or to assess how much value will be added by an acquisition. Investing in areas of the business that create returns in excess of their cost of capital will increase value. Investing in a business that doesn't will reduce value. The results may need careful handling: managers who thought they were running profitable businesses can react badly to the news that they are actually destroying value. The analysis is a vital contribution to the debate over where and how to focus resources in order to add the greatest value.

It is just as important to obtain an understanding of the profitability of current products, channels, markets and customers in order to:

- ensure that costs are not incurred where the return is less than the cost; where this is the case, actions to change the mix of products and customers may be necessary to provide positive cash flows which can re-invested in the business – either in new product development, IT, machine tools and so on – or paid as dividends to shareholders
- focus resources on developing the right products through the right channels to the customers where the relationship is known to be profitable.

It is in this area that ABM provides the highest-quality information to support decision-making.

Value Based Management seeks to build a performance measurement system focused on enhancing shareholder value. If well designed, integrated with other measures such as ABM and BPM, and fully understood by management at all levels, it provides a solid foundation for improved performance.

## ABM AND CUSTOMER RELATIONSHIP MANAGEMENT

In the Introduction to this book, the key role of ABM in supplying the missing dimension of profitability was introduced as the vital aspect of Customer Relationship Management (CRM). Is CRM anything new? Organizations have always had to consider customers, so why raise the relationship with them to the level of being a new discovery at the start of a new century?

The key change at the turn of the century was the ascendancy of the Internet as the route to provide access to almost anything, and from the comfort of your own home, or conveniently (some argue), from anywhere via your mobile phone. At the same time as the Internet became an important channel to market, the market itself went through radical change: global markets, 24/7 service levels, changes from monopoly supply to competition in sectors such as telcos and utilities, and the spectacular rise and equally spectacular fall of many dot.com businesses.

In all this turmoil of change, when the ground rules of business seem to be rewritten on a weekly basis, some fundamental aspects of business do not change, although they are regularly forgotten. In the rush for market share, are telcos forgetting the longer-term impact on profitability of capturing customers with characteristics that will seriously erode profitability? In the rush to provide products via a Web site, are financial services companies encouraging customers to perceive products as commodities where hunting for the cheapest is the primary use of the technology? In the rush to offer a range of products and services on the back of the primary relationship, are utilities companies risking loss of the primary business if customers are unsatisfied with the fringe services? In the rush to offer an exciting and convenient Web-based sales channel, are some dot.com distribution businesses forgetting to put in place rigorous, accurate and timely back-office and distribution processes? All these questions are at the heart of CRM.

The real pressure on businesses stepping into the world of e-commerce is that customers know that the unit costs of the e-channel are lower, and therefore expect such cost reductions to be reflected in lower prices. In the world of e-commerce, margins will still remain squeezed, so the need to thoroughly understand the costs of processes and the costs that customers create for the business grows in importance. The danger arises when the focus of CRM is only on the sales interface, with sophisticated analysis tools to match revenue to customer attributes of lifestyles, buying preferences and behaviours. ABM is thus the fundamental tool for understanding the behaviour of costs – the missing dimension that should be in place as part of any properly structured CRM programme.

## KEY POINTS

- For ABM to be a success, it must be seen and used in a broader context – one that provides room for other tools from other tool kits to be integrated into the overall approach.

- ABM and Business Process Re-engineering (BPR) are two sides of the same coin of corporate improvement. The common ground is 'activities'. The difference is one of emphasis. ABM tends to start with a focus on products and customers. BPR starts with analysis of processes. One leads naturally into the other, whichever the starting point.

- Value Based Management (VBM) is an approach to measuring the performance of a business, setting targets, and finding and acting on the key levers that increase value. ABM provides the highest-quality information to help pull the right levers.

- Customer Relationship Management (CRM) runs the risk of using sophisticated analysis tools to match revenue to customer attributes of lifestyles, buying preferences and behaviours. ABM is the fundamental tool for understanding the behaviour of costs – the missing dimension to derive customer strategies based on profitability.

# Part III
# Case Studies

# 10 How ABM made a difference: lessons from case studies

The catering business example in Chapter 6 demonstrated how costs flow through an ABM model. For all ABM models, the principles are the same, although the detailed construction of the model is tailored to address the particular issues the business is attempting to resolve. Detailing how an ABM model was constructed for a range of organizations is not particularly enlightening. However, taking a broader view of how ABM made a difference to the performance of organizations demonstrates how powerful the ABM approach can be in focusing management on taking the right actions. In this chapter, we explore how ABM made a difference to a range of organizations. These are based on real-life examples, and build on the author's own experiences.

Starting with some simple examples that illustrate how the ABM approach brought new insights into the real behaviour of costs in an organization, the case studies then move into more complex illustrations of how ABM can make a fundamental difference to business performance. Each case study concludes with the particular lessons learnt, which should be borne in mind in any ABM analysis.

Features of each of the case studies could exist in your own organization. At the end of this chapter, spend a few moments listing the issues your organization faces, with a view to applying ABM to analyse the situation. The issues may concern *positioning* – in other words, product and customer mix, pricing and profitability. Alternatively, the issues may have more to do with *capability* – in other words, finding the scale of process failures, and improving methods and procedures or improving the budgeting mechanisms. In most cases, organizations conclude that they are experiencing a mixture of all these issues, though there is a generally a particular requirement to focus on positioning issues first, followed by changes to capability.

# A MANUFACTURING COMPANY
## DISTORTIONS CAUSED BY COSTING USING OVERHEAD RECOVERY RATES

A component manufacturing company was delighted with its popularity, measured by the consistently high number of requests for quotations that it received from prospective clients. The requests covered a wide range of types of machined component. It was also pleased that it always had a reasonable order book, albeit full of small jobs. Disappointingly, it failed to gain most of the large jobs, so a number of machines for such work, in which they had invested some years ago, tended to be idle for long periods. Although everyone was busy, this level of activity was not reflected in overall profitability: it was drifting dangerously low. Adjusting prices upwards was not an easy solution for the Board, as competition was seen as fierce.

Traditionally, the company used a costing mechanism based on using an Overhead Recovery Rate calculated on an historic ratio of direct material costs to total overheads. There was a suspicion that this approach no longer reflected the real cost to produce various types of component. ABM was seen as the ideal approach to unravel the real behaviour of costs in the business.

The ABM analysis exposed the real cost differences between large and small jobs. Unequivocally, the activity in the overhead departments was proportionately much higher when preparing and producing small jobs compared to large ones. On reflection, this was understandable, as the nature of the work had changed over the years, and customers had become more demanding. Technology had introduced complexity in the overhead departments while reducing unit costs in production.

By properly reflecting the correct level of overhead costs in its quotations, the actual costs of large jobs were seen to be less than in previous calculations. This brought about a change in prices, so the proportion of large jobs increased as these became competitive. This volume increase also absorbed the spare capacity of the manufacturing equipment bought originally for large jobs. Interestingly, although the increased costs for small jobs were reflected in increased prices, this did not have a great impact on the volume of work. These small jobs were so under-priced originally that many customers still stayed with the company. The balance of really unprofitable small jobs and the associated manufacturing machinery were hived off to competitors.

The traditional costing approach had clearly failed to reflect the increased complexity of the overhead activity associated with the size of the job. Also, the effect of having spare capacity had not been considered properly. Capital, here in the form of fixed assets, had to provide a return. The contribution from one type of job had been funding the cost of the spare capacity available for another type of job. The new pricing mechanism brought in work to fill the spare capacity, so the issue of a potentially poor investment was averted. However, had this not been possible, then selling the assets would have been the best option.

Previously, the salesforce thought volume was the key to success, whereas profitability was the issue. Re-training the salesforce to understand how costs were really incurred was the key to reversing the downward trend in profitability.

## LESSONS LEARNT

- Traditional product costing using overhead recovery rates dangerously skews prices when overheads become a significant proportion of total costs.

- Spare capacity (people, space, assets) should be seen as a sustaining cost. Spare capacity is an investment for a future return. If there's no expected return, then remove the capacity and reduce costs.

- The salesforce should be made aware of those factors that drive profitability, otherwise it can become the key factor in bringing down the business.

# A MANUFACTURING COMPANY
## UNDERSTANDING OVERHEADS MAKES A REAL DIFFERENCE TO PRODUCT COSTS

Traditionally, Manufacturing was seen as a department that produced long runs of products. Raw material and direct labour were seen as the predominant costs. Other manufacturing overhead costs were treated as insignificant and were recovered as a flat percentage of the unit production time. However, as the company became more responsive to market demands and also focused on reducing finished-goods stock, the scheduling of work into production changed its characteristics. An ABM analysis was undertaken to find the real constituents of product costs.

In one part of the analysis, Products A and B were compared. Each had the same material cost and item production time. The main difference in production method was the number of set-ups. Product A fell into the traditional category of large batch runs, while Product B was made at different times in smaller batches. For a total quantity of 1000 items, the manufacturing times were as shown in Figure 10.1.

For Product A, the activity of 'manufacture' had the cost driver of volume (number of parts). For Product B, the significance of set-up time meant that two cost drivers had to be considered, 'number of set-ups' and 'number of parts'. When applying ABM, a view had to be taken as to the materiality, or significance, of the activities. Should activities be amalgamated and one cost driver be used or should the significant sub-activities be explored to see whether there were different cost drivers that should be considered? Throughout an ABM analysis, each case had to be considered on its merits.

|  | Product A | Product B |
|---|---|---|
| Set-up time | 10 mins | 10 mins |
| No. of set-ups | 1 | 10 |
| Total set-up time | 10 mins | 100 mins |
| Batch size | 1000 | 100 |
| Total quantity produced | 1000 | 1000 |
| Total item production time (1 minute each item) | 1000 mins | 1000 mins |
| Set-up as % of production time | $\frac{100 \times 100}{1000} = 1\%$ | $\frac{100 \times 100}{1000} = 10\%$ |

**Figure 10.1**    The impact of set-up times

| Product E | Product F | | | | | |
|---|---|---|---|---|---|---|
| Activity | Cost | Cost driver (CD) | CD volume | Cost | CD volume | Cost |
| Machine parts | £800 | No. of machine hours | 300 | £600 | 100 | £200 |
| Set-up machine | £300 | No. of set ups | 5 | £100 | 10 | £200 |
| Collect from stores | £80 | No. of stores visits | 6 | £60 | £20 | |
| Raw material | £1000 | Actual used | | £600 | | £400 |
| Total | £2180 | | | £1360 | | £820 |
| | | | No. made | 5440 | | 410 |
| | | | Cost each | £0.25 | | £2.00 |

**Figure 10.2**  Assigning costs using cost driver volumes

In another part of manufacturing, two products, E and F, were analysed, as shown in Figure 10.2. The cost driver volumes for each activity for each product were used to calculate the costs of each product.

The traditional costing method used the ratio of overheads to direct labour in order to recover overheads: (£300 plus £80) divided by £800. In other words, £0.475 of overhead costs were added to each pound of direct labour. For Product E, this gave rise to a product cost of direct labour £600 plus overhead (0.475 times £600) plus raw material £600 = £1485. For Product F, it gave £200 plus (0.475 times £200) plus £400 = £695.

Using ABM, Product E was shown to be 9 per cent over-priced, while F was 15 per cent under-priced. Using the old pricing method, significant increases in product volumes for Product F would have caused a serious drop in profitability, while Product E would have been priced uncompetitively.

After manufacturing the products, other activities in the business were associated with servicing the customer. In one period, Customer X placed 50 separate orders of 20 items for Product E, making a total quantity ordered of 1000. Customer Y placed one order for Product F for delivery in one quantity of 1000. Although both total quantities were the same, the cost driver of 'the number of orders' was significant in terms of understanding the cost of servicing Customer X. The traditional recovery of the customer servicing overhead costs based on the total factory costs shipped to each customer would have loaded Customer Y with the largest proportion. This is just the opposite of the reality of how costs were being created by each customer.

123

## LESSONS LEARNT

- When considering a proper assignment of overhead costs, it is important to determine which costs are significant and will have a material impact on the product costs.

- Traditional allocation of sales-related costs based on sales value entirely obscures the true nature of the relationship with customers.

# A PRINTING COMPANY
## TUNNELLING DEEPER UNCOVERS THE REAL DRIVERS OF COST

In a printing company the ABM analysis demonstrated how care was required when analysing the activities and their drivers. The company had two types of product. The mainstream product range was based around its traditional production of simple lined writing pads. Two years earlier, it had taken a strategic step to get into the printing of multi-coloured monthly magazines. Newsagents' racks were filling up with journals to cater for every conceivable taste in terms of hobbies, interests and entertainment. The company became concerned when it noticed that profitability changed as the mix of products changed. As it increased the range of its so-called 'high-margin' magazines, overall profitability started to decline.

For nearly twenty years, the mainstay of the company had been the production and printing of writing pads. In those days, it had a simple costing mechanism for quotations whereby it added a standard percentage of the direct labour content to recover overheads then added in direct materials plus a standard profit margin.

Given the emerging concerns over profitability, the company decided to use an ABM approach to provide real visibility of the costs in the company, the relationships between costs, activities and products, and what was driving costs. At the start, it decided to keep the analysis at a high level. For example, in a typical department such as Purchasing, the resources of salaries, space, utilities, IT and so on were shown on the ledger. The key activity was deemed to be 'purchasing', and the driver of the activity was deemed to be 'orders raised'. The number of orders raised was the driver volume. The total activity cost divided by the driver volume gave the unit cost of raising an order; in this case, £10 000 per month was the total cost, and 500 orders raised per month was the driver volume. On this basis, the unit cost was £20 per order. At first sight, this was seen as useful data. To calculate the purchasing activity costs for each product, the company had only to apply the unit cost across the products on the basis of the number of orders it had to place to produce each product. However, the staff felt the analysis was too crude as it masked what was really happening.

Further analysis showed that a key difference in workload occurred when a new item was introduced, compared with the work to just raise follow-on orders for the same item. By analysing the different types of work in the Purchasing department, the unit cost to raise a follow-on order was found to be £7.50, while the unit cost for obtaining quotes and raising orders for new items was £70.

The staff also said that the work associated with magazines took up more time and used more resources than when handling the requirements for writing pads. When these activities were assigned to the product types, the real issue

125

surfaced. The nature of the work involved in organizing the magazine production on a monthly basis was quite different to the traditional work in the past. At the product level, the unit cost to obtain quotes and raise orders for the writing pads was found to be £33, and for magazines a hefty £85.70.

The work in Purchasing was found to be sensitive both to the type of orders being raised and product type. This information was crucial in establishing the real costs of each product type and the impact of introducing new products to the range. Following the discovery of this sensitivity in the Purchasing department, the analysis of activities and their drivers was taken to a more detailed level in all the departments. Having seen the data from the ABM model, Purchasing department staff were keen to propose a number of ways to reduce the unit costs. They considered more call-off contracts with suppliers, more use of IT to link with suppliers, and a rationalization of the supplier base, with less frequent but larger orders being processed.

## LESSONS LEARNT

- The more complex businesses become over time, the more sensitivity is required in the ABM model to reflect this complexity.

- Establishing the appropriate level of 'granularity' of the analysis is the key to drawing out insights that point to where improvements in performance can be achieved.

# A FINANCE COMPANY
## BREAKING OUT ONE-OFF COSTS FROM RECURRING COSTS

A finance company in the City handled deals on behalf of its customers.

From the point of the company's formation, its pricing policy for a new customer was based on a simple price per deal handled. This had been expedient for the company, and simple for the customers to understand. The formula was derived from:

(Total annual costs plus a margin) divided by (Number of deals last year) = Price for the customer

The company believed that it could work out the cost it was likely to incur simply by forecasting the number of deals a customer wanted the company to handle. For projected high-volume customers, the company also gave a discount for the volume of deals. At the end of one particular year, the company just broke even. This surprised it, as it had projected a higher profit given the forecast volumes. In the absence of any better information, the company thought the simplest approach to become profitable again was to increase its profit margin in the costing formula. But market forces indicated that this strategy would just lose business.

Anecdotally, both staff and management knew that some customers were more complex, demanding and rigorous in terms of their needs than others. Only a thorough analysis of the costs of different customer relationships would expose the real cost of doing business. An ABM analysis indicated that some customers, both high- and low-volume, seemed to lock up all the resources in the office when setting up deals. These customers were being under-charged, as setting up each deal cost more than handling it. At the other end of the spectrum, some of the low-volume business was very easy to set up and handle. Could the simple pricing structure be creating prices that were too high in some cases, and thus keeping more simple business away? It also struck someone that if the trend in the mix of customers was changing in a particular way, the company would plunge into a loss.

The simple costing system had not reflected the relationship between the customers' needs and the resources to meet those needs. Just changing the margin on each deal handled would not have solved the problem, as that did not reflect the nature of the work being done to handle a deal. The key was to understand the different work content involved, and match this to the customers' requests when quoting for the work. The ABM data facilitated the dialogue with customers to introduce the new pricing mechanism. Although the ABM model introduced a lot of sophistication in the pricing structure, it was decided that a commonsense approach, highly visible to the customers, would forge a higher

127

level of trust. The set-up costs for deals were set at two price levels: simple and complex. To handle the deals, a fixed price per deal was used.

## LESSONS LEARNT

- Whenever possible, pricing different types of work for customers is more likely to ensure a profitable relationship overall.

- An open pricing mechanism, visible to the customer, is the cornerstone to building a trusting relationship.

# A TRADING COMPANY
## THE COSTS OF DIFFERENT CUSTOMER RELATIONSHIPS VARY

A trading company sold a range of products from stock. The direct costs, essentially the cost of the goods purchased by the company for stock, were known accurately. The main overhead department, with most of the people in it, was concerned with taking orders. A rough-and-ready analysis in the past had shown that the total costs of the department divided by the number of orders gave a cost of £18 per order. Using this figure, they worked out the cost of processing each customer's total orders for a given period by forecasting the number of orders they would be placing. However, staff had noticed that the pattern of work seemed to change depending on the customer and the type of order they placed. They decided to use ABM techniques to understand the relationship between the work they did and the orders they received.

The main activities in the department were broken down into taking orders, checking stocks, and chasing the warehouse to see where a particular item was. The latter activity was usually prompted by the customer, trying to get their order before the original delivery date. The staff then divided their time into the three main activities.

From their records, the staff then looked for the key variable – the cost driver – that caused the activities to occur. These were 'number of order lines', 'number of urgent orders' and 'number of orders'. They looked at historical data to find the volume of these drivers in total, and divided the total activity cost associated with each driver by its driver volume. This gave the 'cost per unit cost driver'. By using the cost driver volumes for each customer, the overall costs could now be assigned to each customer on the basis of 'Cost per unit cost driver' multiplied by 'cost driver volume' for each customer. When the ABM answer was compared with the simple costing method, significant differences in the costs per customer appeared. In particular, the real cost of dealing with one company was now exposed. As the company did not wish to have customers subsidizing each other it introduced a differential pricing mechanism to reflect the different level of overhead activity that each customer created in the Sales Order department.

At the end of the exercise, it was very clear to the company that choosing a very high-level cost driver, 'total volume of orders', gave erroneous results. If the simple costing method had been used, then a change in the volume and mix of customer orders would have plunged the business into unprofitability. In the past, when these adverse trends occurred, the company had little idea of why they had happened. The ABM model also highlighted where change of methods in the way orders were handled would benefit the business. An improvement in delivery performance reduced the level of activity concerned with chasing production. In other words, a reduction in cost driver volumes led to a reduction in the activities linked to the cost driver. The cost drivers linked 'cause and effect' in a way that directly highlighted where a process improvement in one part of the business would reduce costs in another part.

## LESSONS LEARNT

- Understanding the relationship with customers, particularly the costs they create in the business, is fundamental to deciding whether the relationship is, and will continue to be, profitable.

- Once an activity analysis makes the processes transparent, actions to avert unwanted activities lead to significant cost reductions.

# A FAST-MOVING CONSUMER GOODS COMPANY
## ACTIVITY DATA CAN HIGHLIGHT PROCESS FAILURES

A fast-moving consumer goods company faced hard competition and saw a need to drive down costs continually. The fortunes of the company appeared to be in the hands of a declining number of buyers as the major multiples and retailers increased their purchasing power. The company had mistakenly believed that its consistent hard work would achieve an ideal world. In this ideal world, the activities of materials intake and production would be driven by the forecast up to the finished product storage point. Sales orders would remove stock to distribute the products to the customers, who would then be invoiced and pay on time. Marketing efforts would influence the consumer, and the controlled pull-through would determine that the production schedules would just meet demand at planned capacity. Planning would calculate the cost trade-off between holding finished goods stock and the cost of line changeovers. Using Material Requirements Planning (MRP), suppliers would be scheduled to deliver raw materials, containers and labels just in time to meet the production needs. Unfortunately, the reality was far from this ideal.

Planned output levels had been achieved at a premium cost of overtime or additional shift working. The raw materials store overflowed with materials that were not required due to late schedule changes. Materials that had not arrived on time or had been rejected on arrival often caused schedule changes. Everyone concerned with bringing materials into the company or scheduling production blamed poor forecasting as the reason for using their own judgement to determine what they believed actually needed to be produced. Applying such judgements unilaterally, though well-meaning, served only to compound the problems.

As a result, production lines designed for long runs were now expected to produce small batches of urgent out-of-stock lines. The Sales department was still receiving accolades for rushing in with late orders, but nobody was forewarned. The Maintenance departments were fire-fighting breakdowns and wondered whether they would ever be able to start using their preventive maintenance schedules that had been prepared years before. Some products failed quality checks, packaging did not arrive on time, lines broke down, customers changed their schedules, the stock records were inaccurate, pallets were in the wrong part of the country, and the computer was offline for a software upgrade. A typical day was described as starting with a new product trial to be run, the packaging supervisor off sick, the budget amendments overdue, finished goods out of stock, and wrong-day deliveries made to customers. In fact, for as long as most people could remember, this was just business as usual.

131

Like many fast-moving consumer goods companies, a large proportion of total throughput was based on forecasts rather than make-to-order. Conflicting pressures existed that corrupted the accuracy of forecasting. In the absence of credible forecasts, everyone defaulted to their own intuitive feel for the trends. Planning second-guessed the Brand Managers, Buying second-guessed the Planners, and Production second-guessed the Planners. When enough stocks of everything exist, production can always adapt to the latest schedule, however frequent the changes. But the pressure on work-in-progress rapidly reduced the likelihood of the schedule matching the availability of materials, piece parts and packaging. What got into the finished goods stores was the result of making what could be made, rather than those products that would meet the customers' needs.

To compound the problem, the new IT system had been designed on the basis that the whole flow through the business would work without a hitch. This confidence had been taken to the point where an invoice on the customer was raised at the time the order was received. As 50 per cent of the deliveries were not complete to order, this meant that 50 per cent of sales ledger transactions were credit notes. This had become a significant threat to relationships with customers, however attractive the prices of the products were.

The ABM project was originally designed to gain a better understanding of the product costs, a typical requirement for a fast-moving consumer goods business. However, the activity data quickly highlighted the underlying problems, particularly when the activities were shown in the key business processes. None of the key processes operated in isolation: each depended on the outcome of the others. Few people in the organization were in a position to take a process view, but the ABM model clearly demonstrated how the failures at the start of the process created an ever-growing proportion of diversionary activity downstream in the processes. With so much unnecessary activity taking place, it was pointless to develop accurate product costs until the root causes of process failures had been identified and actions to remove the problems implemented. Within four months, the company had reduced its cost base by over 20 per cent, increased its rate of introducing new products, and slashed its product introduction cycle. Further, customer service levels were consistently at a record high. Although customers had always insisted that prices were the key issue, they now acknowledged that buying decisions also included recognition of the whole relationship and the ancillary problems that the supplier had caused through part deliveries, late deliveries and poor invoice accuracy. Through ABM, the foundation for a partnership relationship with its major customers was established.

Crucially for this business, its major customer had embarked on an ECR (Efficient Consumer Response) programme. The ABM work fitted perfectly with the ECR work, as it gave complete visibility of the supply chain across both companies.

## LESSONS LEARNT

- ABM, though ideal for accurate product costing, is also a powerful approach to understanding processes and the links between functions that drive costs from one to another.

- Price isn't everything. Customers place a value on every type of relationship with a supplier.

# A RETAIL CHAIN COMPANY
## A FLAWED INTERNAL CHARGING MECHANISM CAN HAVE SEVERE CONSEQUENCES

The company's main business was selling pharmaceutical and health care products through a diverse range of retail outlets. Some were large stores in main cities, ranging down in size to small outlets squeezed into the centre of towns. To maintain a high brand profile, the company wanted to ensure that it had a market presence in nearly every town in the country, and thus lock out competitors.

In Head Office, one division, Retail Floor Planning, provided a service to all retail branches. The division designed and co-ordinated both the setting up of any new stores and the upgrading and refurbishment of its existing large property portfolio. The main work of the division was architectural design, liaising with planning authorities and organizing contractors to do the refurbishment and fitting-out work. The usual practice of the division's accountants was to charge the Retail Floor Planning division's costs to the Retail Stores division at a rate of 10 per cent of the total cost of refurbishing the branch. The total costs included the Floor Planning division's time, the sub-contractor store-fitters' time, and the actual materials used. This 10 per cent charge was seen as the Floor Planning division's 'income'.

As long as the total income for the year covered all the costs, and left a little 'profit', nobody in the Floor Planning division worried about the charging mechanism. However, a number of issues had surfaced within the company. Over the years, the mix of sizes of stores being refurbished changed, so the 'income' to the Floor Planning division from the Retail Branch division declined. This worried the divisional accountants, who wanted to increase the charge rate. Resentment over this issue from a number of branches had reached Board level. The Retail division felt that some branches were 'paying through the nose' and value for money was poor. The strength of feeling had created rumours that the Floor Planning division should be outsourced in its entirety. To resolve the issue, a basic ABM model was constructed to find:

- the actual activities undertaken to provide the planning service

- the attributes of each retail store project that determined the mix and level of activities.

It was accepted that the direct costs of sub-contractors and materials would still be allocated to each individual store project. These costs would be visible and independent from the work done by the Floor Planning division. The analysis showed that small branches required a disproportionate amount of planning activity, compared to large branches, as shown in Figure 10.3.

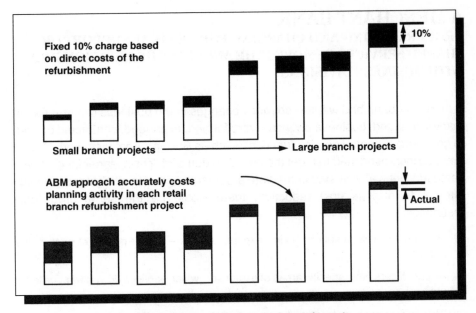

**Figure 10.3** Old and new basis to assign costs

Once the contractors' costs and materials had been taken out of the equation, the key cost driver for the actual planning activities was found to be branch size. The smaller the branch, the greater the real work of the Planning division. Small outlets squeezed into high street locations always had more difficulties to resolve in terms of technical hazards and local authority conditions. The proposed charging mechanism worked in the opposite way to the previous charging mechanism! When the activities within the Floor Planning division were fully analysed and all the key cost drivers found, the ABM data was then used to make accurate estimates of any planned work. The visibility of the costs and drivers in the model also gave the Retail division confidence that it was getting value for money. Once the costing system had proven credibility, the branches then admitted that the quality of the service was, in fact, very good.

## LESSONS LEARNT

● Finding the right cost driver for activities is fundamental to understanding the dynamic behaviour of costs.

● In most guises, cross-charging sows the seeds of much dissent and resentment between functions. An ABM analysis makes the real relationship between functions visible and credible, and provides a proper basis for charging.

# A MERCHANT BANK
### PROPER COSTING AND CHARGING FOR CENTRAL SUPPORT OR SHARED SERVICES REMOVES THE ANGST IN THE RELATIONSHIP WITH BUSINESS DIVISIONS

A merchant bank had weathered many changes in the business climate. As the market changed, business divisions were formed, expanded, contracted or sold. In good times, central service functions such as Building Administration, IT, and Finance increased staff to meet the growth in demand. Yet in leaner times, these same functions always had immediate arguments against belt-tightening. In any attempt to discuss cost reduction, there would be the same predictable responses;

> I've only got five people checking expense claims – I can't get rid of even half a person!

> All our officers have specific areas of expertise – which services do you want us to cut out?

> We can't cut back on the Help Desk – the users would crucify us!

Since the Business divisions' bonuses depended on profit after deductions of Central Services' charges, divisional directors bargained hard against each other to reduce their own share of the re-charged costs. Some of the more entre-preneurial divisions even began levying service charges on each other. All this charging and re-charging served only to distract managers from the real debate about growing the business that should have been taking place. The questions that never seemed to surface were: 'What creates the need for the service, and how much of it?', 'How cost-effective are these various services?' and 'What are they worth to their divisional customers?'

Introducing ABM was a turning point in resolving both failures in current charging practices and the declining relationship between the Business divisions and Central Services. The key aspects to get right within the ABM model were the service outputs from the Central Services functions, and the measures for assigning output costs to the Business divisions. The measure for each output had to meet two stringent criteria:

- It had to be accepted as fair and equitable by all receivers of the service.
- It had to be controllable by each division receiving the service.

The focus of debate thus shifted first to choosing the measures, then to reducing the unit cost of each service. In the past, if total demand for a service fell, costs stayed the same, so unit costs rose. Now, service managers became account-able for the cost of the spare resource. They could channel it into another service where demand was increasing, or eliminate it, usually through natural wastage.

Initially, some departments found the accountability for spare resource hard to come to terms with, particularly IT, with a number of under-used legacy systems. However, in IT, the principle of highlighting spare resource also exposed a large, untapped pool of developers' time which divisions had requested in the budgeting season, but later decided not to use. The cost of this had previously been lost in the morass of full absorption costing and re-charging. Under the new rules, IT management became much more proactive in scheduling this scarce and valuable resource.

A year after these principles were adopted, service costs had fallen by over 20 per cent, a considerable sum. The cost debate continues each year, but now on a much sounder footing. Despite the cost savings, service quality actually increased, as managers of the service functions now concentrated on improving processes and further reducing unit costs.

Since the introduction of the ABM approach, a more subtle benefit has emerged. As the visibility of service costs has improved, and the mentality of cross-charging other divisions has subsided, business managers are focusing on the bank's real customers. The ABM model was set on a path to include product and customer profitability in the businesses that dealt with external customers.

## LESSONS LEARNT

- Once again, cross-charging that has no basis in fact or understanding of what is driving what costs significantly clouds the real underlying issues to be resolved.

- While managers are diverted into fruitless argument, little attempt is made to improve the levels of service or reduce unit costs through process improvements.

- Outsourced services, shared services and central HQ services are all typical areas where ABM exposes the real relationships between service providers and service receivers.

# A HEAD OFFICE FUNCTION
## ACTIVITY AND VALUE-FOR-MONEY ANALYSIS CREATE ENHANCED EFFECTIVENESS

The Global Costing Group of a major international corporation, based at its international Head Office, decided that ABM was the ideal approach to analyse other business units. Before launching ABM on others, it decided to test the approach on itself. If ABM could resolve issues in a Head Office function, then it would go a long way to removing any scepticism or cynicism in the business units. The group set itself a number of objectives:

● to improve the value of the reporting process
● to evaluate the usefulness of ABM as a structural approach to managing an overhead department.

The group considered itself as an outside supplier and consultant to the Corporate Head Office and the business units. Its key service was Financial Reporting, and the reports were the 'products'. The customers were Regional Management, World Head Office Management, the Financial Consolidation department, Group Treasury department and all the Country Subsidiary companies. It also had a number of suppliers of service, namely the IT department and the Subsidiaries themselves, which supplied information.

First, the group calculated the direct and indirect cost of maintaining the existence of the staff involved in the reporting process. For each individual grade of person, the costs included salary and employment costs, vehicles, travel and entertainment. Other overhead resources were assigned to people. These costs included rent, power, heating, office furniture and equipment, accounting, training, personnel administration, reception, PCs, e-mail, printers and IT support. This calculation provided a cost per hour for each job grade.

Each member of staff logged how they used their time in a typical month. The categories of activity were identified as shown in Figure 10.4. Staff were surprised at the high percentage of diversionary time that was required. Addressing the root causes of this diversionary time provided the opportunity to enhance their service on their core activities. The activities were then assigned to the outputs from the group. This proved to be very insightful, as it exposed which outputs attracted the most diversionary activity. Much of this was due to the need to check and correct errors in the monthly figures provided by the business units – an instance of the internal customer creating process failures and then resenting being charged for them!

The valuable outputs were treasury reports, financial and management accounts and advice. The value was made up of content (relevance, actionability), accuracy and timeliness (information was a perishable item). There were

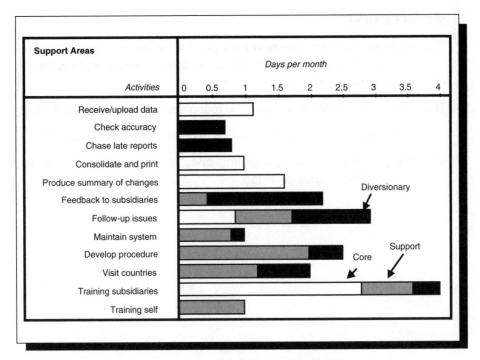

**Figure 10.4** Use of time by activity attribute

support outputs, such as policies and procedures, the reporting system and training. There were also diversionary outputs, such as feedback, corrections and re-submissions. The costs of producing the outputs could now be compared with the value of the reports as perceived by the internal customers. As a result of this action, the group was able to reduce the frequency of reports that cost more than they were worth, or eliminate them altogether. Further brainstorming to change methods resulted in the consolidation of the forecast quarterly only at Regional Office, combining treasury actuals with financial submission, distributing checking software to the field, and rationalizing the chart of accounts and entity names.

Six months after implementation, the transfers to Head Office reduced from two days to two hours, there was a massive reduction in reporting errors, deadlines were beaten by seven days at month end, and became four days monthly thereafter. The group increased capacity by over 30 per cent and, importantly, stress levels reduced. The high turnover in staff the group had experienced was eliminated. Given that such improvements in productivity and effectiveness in Head Office had been rare in the past, the group was able to introduce ABM in the business units by being the first benchmark for the process. The ABM rollout continued without resistance.

## LESSONS LEARNT

- The use of attributes to determine the type of activities is a powerful mechanism to understand where value is being created and where process failures divert people away from their core work.

- The diversionary activities focus on the root causes of the process failures.

- The diversionary activities are the source of potential major cost savings.

- Involving customers, in this case internal ones, is key to making a judgement on the value of the outputs provided.

# AN IT SERVICES DIVISION
## ACHIEVING A PROPER BASIS FOR COSTING AND CHARGING IT SERVICES

Over a five-year period, an international organization had achieved major cost reductions and customer service improvements, in which information technology played a significant part. New systems and technologies were implemented: a client server platform, document image processing, e-mail and remote data logging.

Yet in this period, IT Services' reputation for timely and fit-for-purpose service delivery sank to an all-time low. The costs of IT support and operations were rising inexorably. Users were questioning as never before what they were getting for their money. The management accounts were strikingly uninformative. They showed the cost of IT resources – staff, software, travel and so on – but very little about what those resources were doing or what they delivered to the business. Pressure was growing for IT Services to benchmark its activities and to outsource areas which were shown to be inefficient. But what did it really cost to deliver application systems?

Application costs had been based on a single measurement: computer usage. This had some merits: usage was easy to measure, and for many years had represented the highest percentage of application costs. However, times were changing. Technology was diversifying more and more, and support costs were escalating in step. Specialist knowledge of client/server technology, networking and packaged software now supplemented traditional mainframe skills. For the first time, an ABM analysis revealed the total costs of servicing the user applications. The top six applications are shown in Figure 10.5.

The analysis demonstrated that the mix of costs for the main application systems varied widely. Up to that point, managers had directed their efforts almost exclusively to improving the efficiency of computer usage. The figures now showed that significant leverage on cost reduction could be gained from the support and operational areas. In addition, by making explicit the support and operational costs of ageing mainframe systems (Applications B and D) the true expense of these systems compared with a modern package-based solution (Application F) was exposed. With their new understanding of the relative costs, managers justified replacing the legacy systems and realizing the promised savings, as they now knew how and where costs were incurred. Application C, the Geographic Database, used data plotters which required high levels of support for servicing and replenishing ink and stationery. Once the support costs were exposed, the case was made for progressively replacing the plotters. Drawings from the new equipment were produced more quickly and with greatly improved clarity. User satisfaction soared, and overall costs were lower.

141

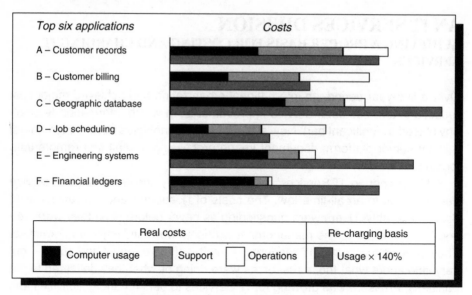

**Figure 10.5**   Cost of servicing the user applications

The re-charging mechanism had fallen into disrepute. Users were asking whether they were getting a fair deal from the IT function's cost recovery method. Re-charges of IT services comprised two elements: computer usage, and an overhead allocation. The computer usage charge was calculated using a complex algorithm that was incomprehensible to those outside IT. The overhead allocation – a crude and massive 140 per cent of the computer usage charge – had long been a bone of contention with users. The ABM analysis provided a comparison of real costs to the previous re-charge method.

From the analysis, it was evident that charges to users did not reflect the real costs of the applications. Nor did charges reflect the differing operational and support demands of business areas using the same applications. Furthermore, costs were being over-recovered: IT Services was effectively subsidizing the rest of the IT department to the tune of £250 000 a year. Placing this information in front of users enabled open and realistic discussions on appropriate charging and on what could be done to improve value for money.

Analysis also showed that the quarterly billing cycle required a high level of manual intervention to compensate for disparate cut-off dates on related systems. Joint IT/user working parties tackled the areas of heavy support and generated numerous ideas for improvements in reliability and reductions in cost. This had the effect of delaying upgrades to mainframe computer hardware costing £180 000. IT managers had long recognized the importance of problem management, both as a learning process and as a means of prioritizing responses, but they lacked basic knowledge about what was going on. For

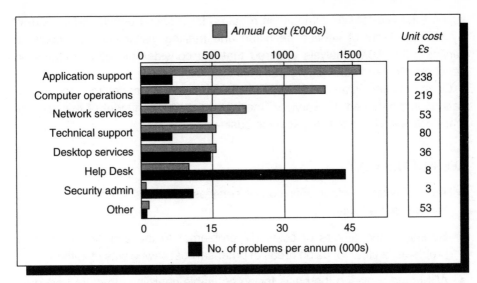

**Figure 10.6** Cost of solving problems

example, to what extent were people throughout the IT support areas engaged in resolving problems? The analysis of the costs of solving problems is shown in Figure 10.6.

It transpired from the ABM model that problem management was costing about £5 million a year, equating to 30 per cent of IT Services' costs. The cost to the company as a whole was even higher, as that sum did not include the costs of service failures borne by user departments or the cost resulting from poor service to customers.

Two factors stood out from the analysis. Firstly, problems resolved by Application Support and Computer Operations cost three to four times more than those resolved by other areas. By investing time in building robust procedures, support costs fell by 20 per cent. Secondly, Help Desk and Security Administration resolved more than half the problems. Why was their problem-solving running at such a high rate? Investigation showed that the recent innovations in information technology were creating turmoil among poorly trained users, who had no choice but to flood Help Desk with cries for help. By providing targeted user training, the volume of calls was almost halved, and the call-queuing time and Help Desk responsiveness were dramatically improved.

Outsourcing and benchmarking were increasingly hot topics for IT Services. But managers were aware that neither was a panacea for their problems. It was unlikely that outsourcing an ill-defined and poorly costed service would yield the expected cost benefits, or at least only at the risk of reduced service levels. Similarly, the company had insufficient knowledge of its services and activities to

143

support the like-for-like comparison required for a sound benchmarking study. By forcing clarity of service definition and making visible the true costs of services, the ABM analysis ensured that the considerable effort entailed in benchmarking and outsourcing was fruitful.

Once the conclusions had been drawn from the ABM model and recommendations implemented, IT Services' management was confident of the benefits that were now visible to the rest of the business.

## LESSONS LEARNT

- ABM provided a clear definition of services, their costs, and the activities involved in their delivery.

- By linking the drivers of costs (IT problems) to the activities to resolve problems, a clear focus on areas of potential cost saving was identified.

- ABM data provided the basis for an equitable charging structure based on actual resource consumption.

- Assessing the benefits of outsourcing and benchmarking can only be achieved if meaningful data for comparison is available.

# A UTILITY COMPANY
## SELLING OFF THE IT SERVICES FUNCTION MEANT
## UNDERSTANDING THE DYNAMICS OF THE NEW BUSINESS

An electricity utility company decided to sell off its IT Services function so that it could become a separate business. It needed to set up a proper business relationship between the two companies. However, the relationship between IT Services and the utility had become more and more fraught. IT managers' time was increasingly dominated by negotiations over budgets for IT staff and estimates of the time required for additional work.

Both parties approached negotiations believing the other to be at fault. The IT managers suspected their opposite numbers of being out to build reputations as tough negotiators by paring IT budgets to the bone regardless of the effects on service quality. The utility's managers, on the other hand, suspected their IT counterparts of retaining too many staff, all of whom had to be charged to the client by fair means or foul.

An exhausting, frustrating and time-consuming process resulted which left all parties dissatisfied with the end result. With the information available, no one really knew whether the resources agreed would meet the likely demand for IT services in the future and whether they would represent good value for money. The IT supplier provided both new development, and operations and support to existing systems. All services were charged to the client at cost, with a percentage margin placed on top.

The resources needed for new developments were agreed relatively easily. Sophisticated project planning tools gave credibility to the numbers reached. Because most new applications were intended to generate additional revenue and development, resources were capitalized rather than being met out of revenue budgets, so a favourable financial calculation usually resulted. Project budgets could therefore be generous. The same did not apply to operations and support for existing systems. Each year, both parties had to agree the budget for services. Any unforeseen work had to be negotiated separately as the need arose. Because much of this work did not produce such a favourable financial outcome, negotiations were often fraught with difficulty. The critical problem facing both sides was that value judgements for operations and support were difficult to evaluate – even though failure to perform certain tasks could put the well-being of the client's business at risk. Costs were the only parameter that managers could debate.

The whole process of negotiation was made more difficult by the pressures placed on both parties. Client managers were required to halt what had been, in recent years, a steady rise in IT operations and support spending. The belief that further increases would deliver little tangible benefit was widespread. Increases,

145

they argued, would simply help shore up an inefficient, over-staffed organization, rather than delivering much-needed improvements in service. IT managers, on the other hand, were under pressure to keep the contract with their
client intact at all costs. Large, long-term contracts were hard to find. It was vital
that the relationship improved.

IT resources were already stretched to breaking point. Problems arising from
an upgrade to a new desktop standard as well as the roll-out of new mainframe
applications meant that some people were already working as many as 70 hours
a week. IT managers did their best to justify their requests, but the financial
arguments supporting the need for more resources were weak. They were
unable to answer the clients' most fundamental questions: what was it essential
to spend; how could the size of the increase be justified; what was desirable but
not essential; where could savings be made? Without a better understanding
of the costs involved, both sides remained unable to reconcile their different
positions. A breakdown in the relationship was just around the corner.

The financial reporting systems originated in the days when IT was simply
an in-house cost centre. They provided accurate costs of all the people within
operations and support, and through a project costing system, the cost of any
separately specified piece of work. However, they gave no clues about the costs
of services to the client, the costs of the component tasks, and the impact upon
costs of the many factors that influenced the level and quality of services. Over
the next three months, as part of an ABM study, each of the key services was
defined and costed. As information began to flow out of the work, the relation-

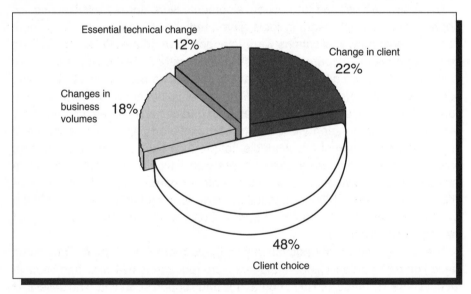

**Figure 10.7** Drivers of IT costs

ship began to improve. For example, the data quickly revealed that 70 per cent of the total costs of operations and support were driven by client requests, as shown in Figure 10.7. Up until then, the client had been haggling over the cost of a Help Desk technician here or a mainframe analyst there. It now began to realize the degree to which its own behaviour had a dramatic effect on costs. Attention on both sides now switched to the nature of the client's requests.

The client changed some part of its organization several times per year, each time resulting in the migration of people and their equipment around the business. In one case, an entire office relocated to a new site. Six months later, due to changes in another part of the business, they relocated back to their original office. The client initiated over 200 investigations into new technology and methods each year. However, 55 per cent of these led nowhere. They were commissioned by different people within the client company. Several ended up investigating the same subject. In an attempt to constrain costs, the client had insisted on allowing only incremental increases in network capacity, usually when someone complained about the poor performance of their machines. In consequence, many small changes occurred, rather than a few large ones.

Fact began to replace emotion, as both sides understood the true cost drivers of operations and support. One outcome was the introduction of a rate card for services, as shown on Figure 10.8. Both parties could now work together on the

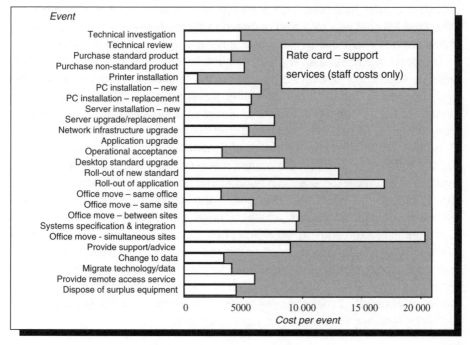

**Figure 10.8** A rate card for IT services

likelihood of future scenarios. Whenever an event occurred, accurate predictions of resources were immediately available. New events would still have to be estimated from scratch, but the estimating process was much easier than before, and less contentious.

Negotiations over IT costs were transformed from antagonistic, long-winded debates about the need for people to positive and brief discussions about the need for activities. This gave the client a real feeling of control over IT spending for the first time. The supplier benefited as well. Given stable prices, a reduction in costs would grow the margin made on services. Opportunities to reduce costs soon followed. Despite attempts to manage rigorously the handling of user problems, far more people were involved in fire-fighting than was first thought. Over 25 per cent of problems recorded within the Help Desk database were referred to people within six or more different departments before a successful diagnosis was made. In each case, the cost incurred swelled to many times that of problems diagnosed swiftly. By improving the user and Help Desk procedures for first-level data collection, the proportion of problems diagnosed rose significantly, halving the costs of problem-resolution. Other insights into cost reduction opportunities followed.

Suppliers for products had always been selected on the basis of price alone. It emerged, however, that three suppliers in particular had a poor record of successful order fulfilment, and a record of delivering poor-quality products. When the full cost was revealed of dealing with the litany of errors, the need to chase delivery and the arguments over payment, all three were dropped.

The costs of problems arising out of unfamiliarity with new *Windows NT* client systems accounted for over 25 per cent of the total cost of problem-resolution. This dropped to under 10 per cent after travelling road shows were commissioned, at the IT supplier's expense, aimed at addressing the most common user problems. At last, with prices stablized through the use of the rate card, the IT supplier could enter into a process of continuous improvement and expect a prize at the end: a growth in the margin made on services. Having suffered the agonies of a cumbersome annual budgeting process, the company was able to rapidly predict the effect that changes in the marketplace would have on IT resources. It began to question whether it needed a budget process at all! Within four months of ABM starting, both sides had a clear understanding of the costs of the activities that made up each of the key services. Negotiations were positive, brief, and focused upon predictions for the root causes of activities. Client managers were able to finely tune their spend by minimizing the root causes within their control. IT managers were able to help them to minimize their spend further by reducing the costs of activities over time.

In the longer term:

- Overall spend declined for the first time since IT was outsourced – a saving of £1m over three years without any drop in service quality.
- Far less time was spent on budgeting.
- A stronger partnership developed between client and provider – allowing them to deliver new services to the end customer more quickly.

## LESSONS LEARNT

- In the absence of cost driver knowledge, negotiations between service providers and receivers will always be fraught with difficulty, with an overlay of emotion and suspicion.

- When service receivers see the impact of their own behaviours on service providers, actions to change such behaviours have a dramatic effect on reducing costs.

- Through using an accurate and mutually agreed rate card for services, accurate predictions of resources immediately become available.

- Once a relationship between receivers and providers of services is understood, the requirement for conventional budgeting evaporates.

- Both parties understood each other's goals and recognized that, with the use of sound activity-based information, they could work together to achieve them.

# A COURIER COMPANY
## THE DEVIL IS IN THE DETAIL, WHICH IS ONLY KNOWN BY THE PEOPLE DOING THE WORK

A courier company delivered packets and parcels all over the world. Its initial strategy had been simple: just go for new markets and volume. The success of the strategy had resulted in over 20 per cent annual growth, which was set to continue. Its expansion plans had been going well, but in a highly competitive market its profit margins were vulnerable to price slashing by competitors. Getting its pricing structure right was seen as being vital for long-term growth and profitability.

At first sight, the overall business process seemed simple. The customer contacted the company and asked for a package to be collected. The package was collected from the customer and taken to a local 'hub', usually located at an airport. At the hub, the package was sorted into the next destination hub. Many destinations were located in other countries. A plane then took the package to the next hub. At the destination hub, the package was sorted to go on a route with other packages to a variety of final destinations. The package was then delivered to the addressee.

Pricing was based on knowing the cost per unit of distance travelled for each mode of transport in each country. The problem the company identified was that even with accurate route distances for each mode of transport, some customers were profitable and others were not. With very small margins and intense competition, the company was fearful of the consequences of increasing volumes of business. Volume could mean plunging into unprofitability. In an effort to try and understand the dynamics of the business, management listed the activities in the key processes. These were:

1. Go to collect from customer's address and pick up package.
2. Return to hub location.
3. Sort package at the hub.
4. Fly package from hub to hub.
5. Sort at second hub for destination route.
6. Drive to delivery area.
7. Deliver to addressee at final destination.

Even though the process looked simple, it was felt that some key element was missing from the analysis. To try to understand the detail of all the tasks, management involved the staff who did the work in each part of the process. The staff came up with a similar list of activities, but with one important addition that management had not been aware of. Where management had the activity 'Go to collect from customer's address', staff had: 'Go to customer's address', but, in addition, 'search for individual'.

The staff knew that collecting a package from a customer was not just a matter of arriving at an address. Much time was spent in searching for the specific individual in the company who had the package to be collected. Sometimes they would arrive at a company's reception area and there would be the parcel waiting on a specially marked-out part of the counter with all the paperwork ready. The collection would only take moments. In contrast, at a particular oil refinery there were six different entrances. At each, nobody was expecting the collection, no parcel was to be seen, and it could take another hour while Security telephoned round the company trying to drag people out of meetings or get the parcel to the right gate. Such a collection threw the whole collection schedule for the day into chaos.

Working with the staff who made the collections, the company created a code to signify the degree of difficulty in finding the person who had the package. The overall costs then had the extra subtlety built into the pricing structure. The company now had two significant 'cost drivers'. A cost driver was defined as the particular variable that had a significant relationship to the costs of the activity. One significant cost driver was 'distance', with a unit cost for each mode of transport, such as motorcycle or plane. The other significant cost driver, based on a code, was 'degree of difficulty' in finding the exact package pick-up point. A third but less significant cost driver was the 'event' that took place to sort a package at a hub. Overall, sorting costs were a small percentage of total costs. The sorting costs were based on each package, and were therefore related to the number of packages collected from a particular customer. The company now had a means of calculating the total delivery cost for each customer.

Armed with the new data, the salesforce was then able to negotiate new prices for customers. Those with a low level of difficulty enjoyed a lower price. Those that attracted a difficulty code which led to a higher rate usually agreed to change their collection procedures, both to reduce courier charges and because the new procedure also saved them time and confusion. Those few customers which refused to change their process and did not want to pay the higher rates moved their business to competitors. Unbeknown to the competitors, the additional volume would be loss-making. With the subtle costing mechanism in place, new and differentiating services were introduced. Each service and customer was known to be profitable by design. The guesswork and associated risk were eliminated.

By using technology, in particular bar-coding, the complete route, and therefore the complete combination of activities and cost drivers, was known at the time a customer's request to collect a package was received. The package carried the information, so the worldwide system knew the forward load to expect at any time and place. As a by-product of this information, customers were able to use the Internet to track where their parcels were in the delivery pipeline. Resources, such as transport and people, could now be planned and scheduled to achieve the balance between competitive customer service levels and an acceptable level of cost. The data also provided a means of modelling the impact of changing the processes and the activities within them.

## LESSONS LEARNT

- To find out what is really going on in a business, ask the people who are doing the work.

- Customers cause many costs in a business. When these costs are exposed to customers they are often more than willing to change their behaviour or processes so that they can benefit from the subsequent cost reductions.

# A MANUFACTURING AND TECHNICAL SERVICES COMPANY
## A SIMPLE PRICING MECHANISM MASKS COMPLEX AND COSTLY CUSTOMER RELATIONSHIPS

A manufacturing and technical services company manufacturing heat-resistant refractory bricks and associated equipment for the metal, glass and cement refining industries was being hit heavily by the effects of exchange rates on its level of exports. It needed to improve profitability quickly without jeopardizing the levels of service to the customer. However, its existing management information did not provide the visibility needed to support urgent commercial and resource management decision-making.

The turning point in the search for ways to improve profitability came when management knew that they were unable to answer some fundamental questions:

● Who are our least profitable customers, and why?
● Which are our most profitable products, and why?
● Can we compete more on price for certain products?
● Which industries and regions should our salesforce focus on?

The pricing policy they had been using worked on a simple basis. The ex-factory cost, made up of direct and manufacturing overheads, for each customer order had 12 per cent added to 'recover' the costs of the central functions. These included the Sales departments and Engineering Customer Services.

The ABM analysis was concentrated on all the ex-factory functions. Costs were assigned in a number of ways to build up a matrix picture of the relationship to all the customers, the products they bought, and the applications the products were used for. This brought to light an entirely different view of how costs were created within the business. The first result of the ABM analysis was an overview of the profitability of the different geographical regions within which their customers were located. The familiar hook curve of cumulative profitability shown in Figure 10.9 showed that the maximum profit of £12m was reduced to £10.8m just based on the profit erosion from several regions. Investigating deeper into each region gave the country and then customer view.

Region M, Southern Europe, was losing the most money. This result confirmed management's suspicion that significant resources were dedicated to a region which had failed to generate significant volumes of business, and was unlikely to do so in the future. The office was closed, delivering an immediate improvement of £0.5m to the bottom line.

Region R, Eastern Europe, was only marginally better. After focusing in on

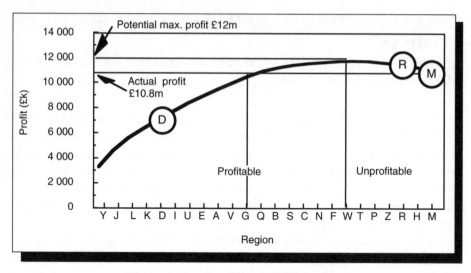

**Figure 10.9** Cumulative profitability by region

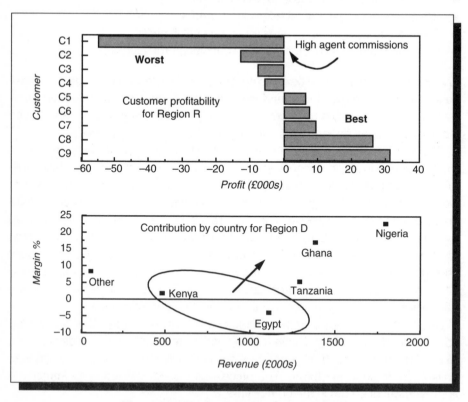

**Figure 10.10** Country and customer profitability

individual customers, as shown on Figure 10.10, it became clear that the total losses from the four worst customers outweighed the gain made from the four best. Due to the nature of the region, business has traditionally been conducted through agents. The agents charged high commissions, and had so far been the focus of a substantial sales and marketing effort.

However, as access to Eastern Europe had improved over the years, agents had been able to represent the interests of more and more companies, many of which were competitors within the same markets. Trading through agents therefore ceased, and a dedicated salesforce was put in their place. As a result, agent commissions disappeared, sales and market spend halved, and levels of business from each of the customers concerned grew.

Region D was in the profitable part of the hook curve. However, when the margin from each country in the region was calculated, questions about Kenya and Egypt were raised. A thorough analysis of the projected sales for Egypt showed that it would be advisable to withdraw from that country. Kenya indicated greater potential, so a higher level of sales input was put in place.

Managers believed that they already had a firm grip on product profitability. They knew that the iron and steel industry overall accounted for a healthy profit. However, they suffered a profound shock when they realized that two of their most highly prized product groups within the industry had been losing money. The blast furnace products were believed to be profitable due to the very low cost of manufacture. Special products, such as continuous casting, were thought to be profitable due to the high prices charged for what was a customized construction and assembly process. However, in both cases considerable Sales and Marketing resources were focused on growing volume and providing technical information. In addition, the salesforce for the blast furnace products was happily cutting prices in an attempt to grow the volume, even when there was little competition present. In the case of special products, both the customers and the salesforce demanded a significant amount of technical support. This was provided by an army of specialist engineers, each one an expert in a relatively narrow field.

The ABM analysis made it easy to challenge Sales and Marketing management's use of resources. As a result, the Sales and Marketing effort changed its focus towards the areas in which it could add most value. In addition, the technical and sales support for special products became a service for which the customer is now charged. Fewer people possessing a broader range of knowledge were provided, and the technical training for Sales staff improved. Finally, investment in additional manufacturing capacity was suspended until managers were confident that the products were profitable and that there were markets to sustain the required profitability for some time to come.

In terms of the impact on business results, within four months they had defined the information that mattered, collected the necessary data, and announced an immediate £0.5m improvement to the bottom line. Further, they finally achieved cost reduction initiatives amounting to 20 per cent of central overhead, the suspension of a £3m investment in products that were losing money, and an increase in the levels of business in their profitable products and from their profitable customers.

## LESSONS LEARNT

- A clear understanding of the profitability of products and customers led to better informed commercial and strategic decision-making.

- Short-term cost savings of over 10 per cent of controllable overhead costs were only made visible through the ABM activity analysis.

- As businesses change over time, so pricing mechanisms need to be challenged. Increasing complexity and changing market conditions were key drivers of additional costs that remained hidden by the old pricing formula.

- Entrenched views and beliefs about the behaviour of costs can often only be challenged by the rigorous analysis required by ABM.

# A WHOLESALE AND DISTRIBUTION COMPANY
## TREATING MAJOR COSTS AS FIXED MASKED THE REAL DIFFERENCES IN CUSTOMER PROFITABILITY

A wholesaler and distributor of a mature product range to the retail sector operated from 60 warehouses nationwide to over 18 000 customers. Over the years, a complex, volume-related pricing and discount structure had built up. The company had always believed that the full range of products to all types of outlet was providing profit. At the gross margin level and overall, the business was profitable, but year on year profit was reducing.

The most visible proportion of operating costs was warehousing and distribution. These costs were generally seen as fixed, so the natural instinct was to rationalize the network as a means of achieving cost reductions. The initial exercise to determine the size and location of the logistics network was based on 'volume throughput' and 'distance travelled' calculations. This gave a first approximation to the level of investment needed – a considerable figure. However, before embarking on a complete investment analysis, management decided to examine outlet profitability. All of the costs to service each outlet were calculated and taken away from the gross margin for the outlet. The figure derived on this basis was the 'ABM Customer Contribution'. A graph of cumulative contribution was drawn, starting with the highest-contributing customer and working across in descending sequence of contribution. This graph is shown in Figure 10.11. The company was surprised to discover that 100 per cent contribution came from the first 30 per cent of its profitable customers. The graph also indicated that 60 per cent of its customers provided a contribution of 115 per cent, while the last 40 per cent provided a negative contribution. The contribution data was compared with the volume throughput data. The single largest customer, based on volume, was found to be a negative contributor!

Although warehousing and vehicle costs might be considered as fixed, in reality they can be varied, albeit on a longer timescale. With a high level of stock being held for many of the negatively contributing customers, the company had to look seriously at the relationship with them. When one customer was approached with the proposal to drop them as a customer or prices would have to rise, the customer took a serious look at all the process interactions between the two businesses. This analysis showed that many opportunities existed for both companies to streamline processes and improve the relationships across many functions. Working with the customer brought the situation back to being a positive contributor. A win–win solution had been found.

One area of the graph where a whole cluster of low-volume negatively contributing customers was found brought into question the need for one distribution centre that was due to be built on the original plan. By moving these

157

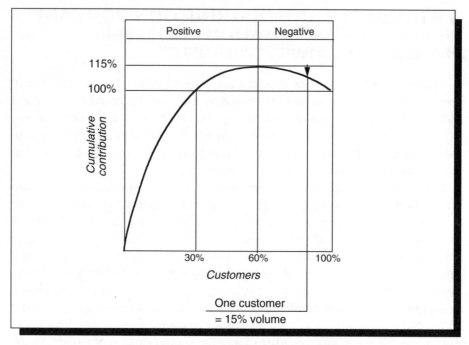

**Figure 10.11**  Cumulative customer contribution

customers to a different distributor, the company avoided over £5m of unnecessary capital investment. Using the ABM data as a key input, the rationalization of
the distribution structure was then based around the profitable customers. The
ABM analysis and increased liaison with customers brought into focus the subject
of ECR (Efficient Consumer Response). The ABM data provided an ideal database to assist in the simulation of alternative levels of service involving advanced
supplier notices, electronic data interfaces and bar-code scanning technology.

## LESSONS LEARNT

- Traditional logistics strategies based on volumes and stock policies can miss
  out fundamental insights concerning the profitability of the customers being
  served. This can be a costly error.

- The transparency of the relationship with customers provided by the ABM
  data gave a firm basis upon which to discuss changing the relationship to
  both parties' benefit.

- When nothing can be done to change the relationship back to a profitable
  one, consider allowing the business to go to competitors. Your own profitability will increase, while that of competitors will fall.

158

# A MANUFACTURING COMPANY
## AN INCREASING NUMBER AND CHANGING MIX OF DISTRIBUTORS ERODED PROFITABILITY

The company manufactured a range of abrasive products that were sold by distributors from a priced catalogue to customers in the car repair industry. It sold the products to its customers, the distributors, at a fixed discount relative to the published catalogue prices used by end consumers. The revenue cascade for the company is shown in Figure 10.12. Manufacturing was the biggest single cost, and had been the focus of management's attention over many years. Many initiatives had been undertaken to improve manufacturing productivity. However, once manufacturing costs had been excluded, customer-facing costs were around 75 per cent of the remaining costs. A number of key issues faced the business:

● There was poor end-to-end visibility of what was driving what inside the business.
● There was a suspicion that some distributors were driving activity in the business to an unprofitable degree.
● Management had lost confidence in the current decision support information.

The company started to use ABM in the manufacturing parts of the business. It

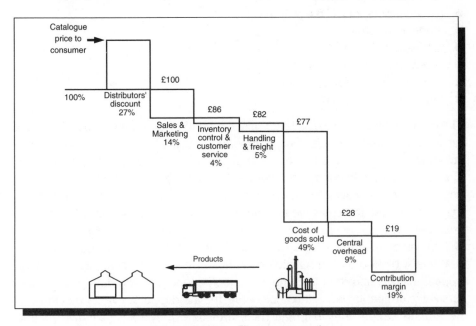

**Figure 10.12    The revenue cascade**

found that products could be described in terms of a number of volume cost drivers. Analysis showed that manufacturing:

- used 23 million m$^2$ of backing material
- used 2.3 million kg of resins
- used 2.4 million kg of abrasive minerals
- used 376 000 hours of direct labour
- created 336 production schedules
- inspected 22 million m$^2$ of finished product
- rejected 372 000 m$^2$
- dispatched 30 000 pallets
- shipped 19.8 million m$^2$ of products.

Knowing the overall manufacturing direct and overhead costs, it used the cost drivers to assign costs to the various products it made. The exercise also refined a number of productivity improvement initiatives. However, when the company looked at the relationship with a typical distributor, it found that it could be characterized by the cost drivers that described the relationship. Analysis of one distributor showed that it had:

- received 16 sales visits
- placed 173 orders
- received 201 deliveries
- placed orders for 2178 line items
- made 21 returns
- received 325 invoices
- received 31 credit notes
- placed 16 emergency orders
- paid, on average, in 63 days.

The data from the typical distributor raised a number of immediate queries. Each function that dealt with distributors reported that they had different cost driver volumes for each distributor. This prompted a thorough survey of all distributors. Cost driver data from each distributor was fed into the ABM model, along with the activities and their costs. By knowing the cost driver volumes for each distributor, the customer-related costs were assigned to each one. Together with the products they took, the overall cost per distributor was found. Comparing the costs with the revenue from each distributor gave the ABM Customer Contribution.

When it plotted the cumulative contribution curve, the characteristic 'hook' appeared. This spurred the company to look deeper into the data. For distributors in the profitable part of the hook curve, the average order value was found to be around £2200, they paid via bank transfers, they had their own product experts to answer customer queries, and they placed accurate orders via an electronic data interchange ordering system. In contrast, distributors in the unprofitable part of the hook curve had quite different characteristics. The average order value was around £150, they had poor payment histories, they raised frequent queries, they had a higher product returns percentage, and they used manual ordering.

The company was initially surprised to discover that average order value size had dropped considerably over the years for some distributors. However, when it first set up the links to distributors, the discount structures had been based on the premise that order values would be high. This had been the case for many years until the network across the country had been expanded and service levels in terms of delivery frequencies increased. Over the years, the impact of these actions had been to erode overall profitability.

The company then pulled the ABM data together by using the process number attributes it had coded to the activities during analysis. First, it looked at the 'order satisfaction' process, as shown in Figure 10.13. From the activity cost data and the cost drivers, it calculated the output costs. As the company was part of a group, it undertook a small benchmarking exercise and discovered that the 'Customer Services' output cost of £15.30 per order was the highest in the group. This was the spur to undertake a process re-engineering review. The activity description of 'process orders' was at too high a level to understand process failures. The activity analysis was taken down to a more detailed level, and the activities then given attributes:

- Review order – Core
- Allocate order lines – Core

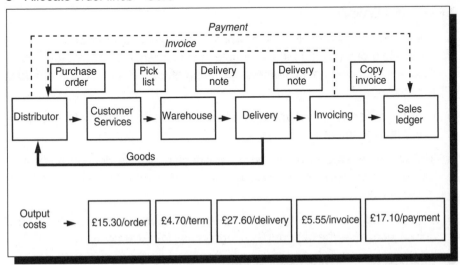

**Figure 10.13**    The order satisfaction process

- Enter data – Support
- Check credit rating – Diversionary
- Resolve queries – Diversionary
- Handle claims – Diversionary
- Staff training – Support
- Transaction reports – Support
- Meetings – Support

When the staff working in the section logged the time they spent on each detailed activity, they were surprised to see how high the diversionary activity was. Some of the issues identified by staff working in the 'order satisfaction' process involved the processes in the Sales departments. When the Sales departments' process was merged into the data, the analysis showed that significant amounts of potential core activity, such as selling, were regularly diverted to handling queries and complaints.

As much of this time was caused by process problems, representatives from the whole process got together to brainstorm the issues. The brainstorming meetings uncovered a typical circular situation. Poor communications between Sales and Administration, with weak IT support, then led to mistakes in satisfying orders, which led to customer queries, which led to diverted sales activity, which led to insufficient time for communications ... and so it went on. The staff found ways to reduce the overall process costs which were then fed back into the ABM model. The ABM model became a central part of the performance measurement system.

## LESSONS LEARNT

- Many companies grow to a point where the original assumptions that led to profitable growth are no longer tenable in the current market. Without visibility of the real costs of customers, the unprofitable relationships are hidden from view.

- Cost drivers and their volumes provide a complete description of the relationship with customers in cost terms.

- The characteristics of a profitable relationship can be defined and transferred to other less profitable relationships. ABM extracts best practice within the organization.

- Using staff to analyse processes in detail and adding attributes for the type of activity quantifies the opportunities for process improvements.

- Unit cost data for processes is the source of data for benchmarking with other parts of the operation or other companies.

162

# A BAKERY COMPANY
## WHEN MARGINS ARE SMALL, DETAILED ANALYSIS IS REQUIRED TO UNRAVEL THE COMPLEXITIES OF MANY DIFFERENT PRODUCTS GOING TO MANY DIFFERENT CUSTOMERS

A bakery had 120 employees, all on one site. Over the years, the product range had grown to 839 products which were sold to a total of 659 customers, ranging from corner shops to large wholesalers. The bakery was profitable, but not comfortably so. The Chief Executive felt that as very little costing or detailed profitability data had ever existed in the business, the time had come to really understand the cost base. The increasing pressure from the major multiple retailers had also focused management's minds on the issue.

The ABM model assigned all costs to all the activities in the business. Manufacturing activity costs, including ingredients, were assigned to products. Product costs were then assigned to customers along with distribution and selling costs. Being a traditional business with many long-serving employees, very little had been written down in the form of product specifications. People knew how many handfuls of ingredients went into various mixes, or had mental algorithms to determine bulk purchasing quantities. The first hurdle was to create bills of materials for each product: for example, how much of what flour went into what dough, and how many loaves or rolls this dough would make. This even involved weighing the eyes of a gingerbread man to see how much icing sugar was used!

The key requirements of the ABM model were to calculate the profitability of each of the manufacturing lines, such as bread, rolls, cakes, sandwich, and frozen, the profitability of various customer groupings, such as major multiples, corner shops, and so forth, and the individual profitability of each product and each customer. A typical analysis for a product is shown in Figure 10.14.

For a customer, the costs included the Sales, Order Processing and Delivery departments' activities, as well as the products that the customer ordered. A typical analysis for a customer is shown in Figure 10.15. For the number of products and customers, the data output from the model was considerable. However, for the bakery's management team, the output proved to be a revelation. After locking themselves away for a couple of days, a number of interesting findings led to some significant changes to their product and pricing strategy. Basically, if the market could not take a reasonable price based on cost, then the product was dropped. Fortunately, there was only one price-sensitive product: the basic sliced white loaf. That product made a healthy profit, so it was a question of adjusting the long tail of previously nil-margin products.

The Chief Executive had a capital expenditure request recently presented to the Board to refurbish the sandwich line. Given the prices they had decided to

**Bread Production Line, product: 800g sliced white loaf**
**Quantity in the period: 503 580**

| Cost element or activity | Total cost | Unit cost |
|---|---|---|
| Self | 885 | 0.002 |
| Flour | 90 874 | 0.180 |
| Emulsified bread fat | 1408 | 0.003 |
| OHM supreme | 2324 | 0.005 |
| Tincol | 1255 | 0.002 |
| Yeast | 2930 | 0.006 |
| Mix the dough | 10 826 | 0.021 |
| Prooving | 7550 | 0.015 |
| Baking | 8181 | 0.016 |
| Cooling | 6052 | 0.012 |
| Unloading line | 12 633 | 0.025 |
| Slicing & bagging | 27 137 | 0.054 |
| Total cost | 172 655 | 0.340 |
| Retail price | 402 864 | 0.800 |

**Figure 10.14**  The cost of a product

| Customer type: Multiple | Customer No.: 251 |
|---|---|
| Activity/Product | Costs |
| Take orders | 962.28 |
| Visit customers | 162.48 |
| Pick & assemble Normal | 5117.47 |
| Pick & assemble Emergency | 853.98 |
| Drive Normal | 4821.08 |
| Drive Emergency | 3926.47 |
| White sliced | 12.53 |
| White whole | 1311.61 |
| Toast A | 12 933.02 |
| Toast B | 10 907.98 |
| Slim | 1601.59 |
| Granary A | 812.37 |
| Granary B | 1790.34 |
| Wholemeal A | 1799.52 |
| Wholemeal B | 4.46 |
| Wholemeal C | 1787.88 |
| Brown A | 1.58 |
| Brown B | 3.83 |
| **Total cost** | **79 563.00** |
| **Total revenue** | **87 320.00** |

**Figure 10.15**  The cost of a customer

charge, sandwiches had been seen as having a bright future. The ABM results showed the line as unprofitable even before selling and distribution costs were added. As the capital expenditure request would have increased production costs, it was withdrawn on the strength of the ABM results. The decision was taken to pull out of the sandwich market, and the bakery sold the sandwich business to a competitor.

Pricing policy had always been based on tradition rather than any knowledge of costs. For example, brown loaves were sold at a higher price than white even though brown flour was cheaper. Also, tradition had determined that they always added around 5p if a loaf was wrapped. ABM showed the wrapping operation was one of the most expensive, and often added 15p to the cost of producing a loaf. They had always thought half loaves were very profitable as they charged more than half the price of a full loaf. In practice, all the costs of producing a small loaf, except the dough itself, were the same as a large loaf, so they were actually the least profitable products.

The company also sold frozen dough in loaf- and roll-size units to customers who then sold shop-baked bread on its premises. In a sense, although this is a popular trend, it is really setting up customers to be competitors. The frozen dough was sold at a pittance, as they had traditionally assumed there was no cost, as it had not been baked. In fact, the mechanized baking was very cheap, but the costs of the freezers was high, so the cost of making frozen dough products was nearly as high as the baked ones. They were in fact subsidizing every loaf that their 'competitors' baked. Needless to say, this issue was brought into the price review.

The bakery had always viewed its large customers with high turnover as the ones to cultivate, and gave them huge sales value discounts. Conversely, it believed that corner shops were just a necessary evil it had to put up with. ABM showed the complete opposite. Many of the large customers were very unprofitable, taking the bulk of the unprofitable products, and demanding high discounts and many deliveries during the day. Many of the small shops were very profitable. The immediate, on-demand and emergency deliveries were phased out, and the discount structure re-designed.

Based on the early success of changing the product mix and pricing strategy, the bakery went on to make further changes that flew in the face of all the years of decision-making based on historical gut feel. Its faith in the ABM model was re-confirmed every month with rapid and high positive impacts on its bottom line results amounting to £1.2m of opportunities, identified with action plans to capture £400 000 of this in the first year.

## LESSONS LEARNT

- Very detailed analysis is necessary to obtain the real costs of a large range of products, and the relationship to a large number of customers.

- An ABM analysis can throw up many surprises, many of them counter-intuitive, and others that fly in the face of traditional custom and practice.

- When the ABM output is acted upon, immediate benefits to the bottom line are obtained.

# A UNIVERSITY
## THE REAL COSTS OF 'PRODUCTS' AND 'CUSTOMERS' REMAINED INVISIBLE IN THE CONVENTIONAL MANAGEMENT INFORMATION SYSTEM

A university had endeavoured to be at the forefront of progress in academic delivery and customer access, encompassing a modular approach to education provision. However, competition for students had become increasingly fierce as universities adopted a more commercial approach. The university needed to make a rapid reduction in costs to match a fall in student numbers, while at the same time improving its service to customers (students) and enhancing its ability to attract more students in the future. This had to be achieved against a background of already stretched academic and administrative resources.

The background to its financial position was common to many in the sector: reducing income from government, and poor growth in student numbers. Other problems in the sector included:

- changes in government policy and an uncertain environment
- the introduction of student loans
- changes in the student profile – for example, more part-time students
- increased competition and marketing sophistication in the university sector
- traditional academic cultural norms – separate power bases of authority in academic faculties, and lack of shared accountability between academics and support staff
- lack of organizational knowledge – there was little visibility of costs or the profitability of different courses and student groups.

Initiatives had already been undertaken to reduce costs, through a 'root and branch' process re-engineering review that identified opportunities to save £1.5m in the short to medium term, as well as considerable scope for longer-term cost reduction and service improvement by improving IT provision and the structure of the curriculum.

A further major opportunity lay in reducing the flexibility of module choice offered to students, by rationalizing the number of modules available and removing duplication. Innovation, whilst being one of the university's greatest strengths, was also inhibiting service. An over-complicated system had developed as a result of the unfettered approach to increasing choice. This resulted in spiralling support costs, an inability to offer the promised flexibility, and a confusing and impenetrable course structure.

To understand the real nature of costs and what drove them, an ABM model was developed to deliver 'module' (product) and 'customer' (student) profit-ability. Total costs of around £68m were first separated into major categories of:

- *Without Income, £8m* – this included infrastructure (such as legal compliance, statutory accounts, corporate management), sustaining (such as strategic planning, marketing and public relations), and internal research.
- *With Income, £21m* – this included funded research, student accommodation, internal commercial services (such as the nursery) and external commercial services (private companies, run by the university).
- *Modules, £35m* – preparing the material and teaching it to students (most costs being within the academic departments).
- *Students, £5m* – activities to support and deal with students (most costs being within the support services departments).

Around 60 per cent of the module costs related to teaching the students. The 'product' cost on a per-student basis varied greatly as this was function of the number of students taking the module. The costs ranged between £200 when 100 students or over took the module, and over £1000 when only ten students took the module. This analysis provided the financial arguments around the issue of module rationalization and choice.

Each department, such as Law or Geography, recruited students and received income per student. However, each student could and did choose a range of modules from a number of departments that built towards their degree. The students also had other support costs that were assigned to them. Using the

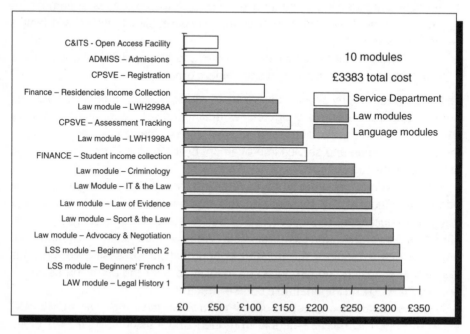

**Figure 10.16**   The cost of a typical Law student

ABM analysis, the university was now able to calculate the actual costs per student and compare this to revenue.

The cost of a typical Law student (out of a total of 13 000 students) is shown in Figure 10.16.

As a result of the combinations of modules chosen, average student costs for each academic department ranged between £3000 and £5000. However, the income per student also varied, based on government policy. The ABM analysis was able to quantify another key issue where, say, a student from the Education faculty, which attracted low revenue, nevertheless chose a broad range of modules from other faculties, many of which were far costlier than modules within Education.

The ABM analysis was able to provide product (module) costing and customer (student) profitability, information that allowed the University to plan its strategy, product development, marketing and use of resources in a similar manner to normal commercial businesses.

## LESSONS LEARNT

- The conventional accounts did not reflect the way in which costs were actually created at the product or customer level.

- With credible data, proper negotiations with fund providers could take place. Previous plans for growth would have plunged the establishment into a heavily loss-making operation.

# AN AIRLINE COMPANY
## SEEING COSTS FROM DIFFERENT BUSINESS PERSPECTIVES HELPS OPTIMIZE CORPORATE PERFORMANCE

An international airline knew how to fly planes. Technically, it had an outstanding record and it was renowned for its cabin service. However, faced with fierce competition it had to be certain that:

- it was functionally effective
- each of its routes was profitable, and the extent of profitability could be measured
- its brands as entities were profitable
- it had formed the right alliances with other airlines.

Functional directors looked at costs, productivity and performance measures. Route directors were concerned with route profitability. In this context, a route, such as London–New York, was a 'product'. Marketing was concerned with brand profitability. In this context a brand, such as First Class, was a 'product'. Network development was concerned with integrating and adding routes, either with the airline's own aircraft, or by forming alliances with others.

For each product, either a route or a brand, costs were assigned for each part of the key process as shown in Figure 10.17.

Brand advertising at the level of the airline's name was treated as an overall sustaining cost, and was not assigned to the products, whereas specific promotions for particular routes or classes of travel were assigned. Lounges and specific check-in areas were assigned to specific brands as an entity, and to routes based on the numbers of passengers on the routes using a particular airport. The facilities and charges at different airports had significant variations, so actual costs, rather than averages, had to be used. All the crew would be route-specific, but proportions of the crew were assigned to brands from a number of routes.

|  | Ticket purchase | Check-in/Departure | Flight | Disembark/Baggage |
|---|---|---|---|---|
| **Direct** | Agent's commission<br>Telephone sales<br>Frequent Flyer | Lounges<br>Check-in<br>Passenger charges | Crew<br>Catering<br>User charges<br>Fuel | Arrivals lounge |
| **Assigned** | Advertising<br>Promotions | Baggage handling<br>Property | Engineering | Baggage delivery<br>Immigration<br>User charges |

**Figure 10.17**  An airline's costs

Each cost element was assigned to a matrix of cost objects in the ABM model. For franchise operations, the ABM model was used to calculate various scenarios, given that charges would feature a mix of fixed and variable costs based on the different cost drivers. Because of capacity issues, such as the maximum number of customers per brand per type of aircraft, care had to be taken to model the non-linear relationships between cost drivers and resources.

In the past, the separate responsibilities for profitability would attempt to maximize their own areas of accountability. Through using ABM, the overall corporate profitability was maximized even where a sub-optimal result occurred at a route or brand level. In particular, the impact of having feeder routes was realized, so a customer's entire journey had to be taken into account, rather than measuring each route as a product. Integrating flight schedules grew in importance, as this was found to be a key determinant of a customer's journey plan and choice of airline.

## LESSONS LEARNT

- Any particular cost can be a subject of interest to a number of different functions. An ABM model can accumulate costs in any number of dimensions to draw out a range of insights about the business.

- The sum of separate functional objectives isn't always the best corporate result (even when this was the intention). An ABM model can draw out the optimum result for the business.

# A POWER GENERATION EQUIPMENT MANUFACTURING COMPANY
## A FOCUS ON PROFITABILITY RATHER THAN VOLUME HIGHLIGHTED PROCESS FAILURES AND BETTER MARKET OPPORTUNITIES

Two years previously, the company had ambitious plans. Production capability was enhanced, it reorganized into high-tech machine cells, a number of new markets were opened up, and a partnership deal with a third-party seller gained access to some lucrative new business opportunities. Unfortunately, as the global recession began to bite, its competitors proved much nimbler, and the order book became perilously weak. What had appeared to be sound capital investments only a few years earlier now showed a poor return.

The business decided that its response would be to 'double the business' within two years. However, the new Chief Executive was adamant that this had to be *profitable* business, achieved without increasing headcount, problems or lead times. Within six months, the company identified process improvements to increase overall capacity by 25 per cent. By analysing product profitability, it decided to enhance its standard products, resulting in fewer 'specials' made to customer order. By analysing customer profitability, it was able to modify its channels to market and revise the mix of customers. The result? A much more profitable mix of products, channels and customers, which doubled profitability – a position that delighted the parent company and shareholders alike.

The problems faced by this company were common to many engineering companies:

- It had no real knowledge of which products and customers were really profitable – only a suspicion that some were, at best, marginally profitable. Product costing on the basis of an Overhead Recovery Rate (ORR) based on the 10 per cent of costs represented by direct labour was the primary cause of major distortions.

- It had a bid-to-order success rate of only 1 in 10 – high selling costs incurred because the business had no knowledge of where best to focus its resources. When lean times came and customers were hard to find, every enquiry was treated in the belief that it would turn into an order.

- Nearly every order was a 'special', even though the company had designed and promoted a standard range of products. As a result, Engineering was involved in every order, consistently resulting in missed delivery dates. Two issues arose. The long lead time from tender to order resulted in many specification changes by the customer at the time of placing the order. The company made every effort to accommodate customer demands while remaining at the original quoted price, for fear of losing the order at the last stage.

- There was no costing information to inform sub-contracting decisions – as a result, internal facilities were poorly utilized while there was a high level of overall sub-contracting. The costing calculation pooled all overheads into the production hourly rate, which provided an erroneous basis on which to compare sub-contractors' prices.

- There were frequent programme changes due to shortages. Attempting to slot orders into gaps in the production schedule for parts and sub-assemblies created re-runs of the materials requirements planning system. Pulled-forward demand now created 'shortages', which in turn drove new programme changes. Instability was built into the scheduling system.

- There were high levels of both inventory and obsolete stock. Inventory was really a measure of many process failures. Programme changes created unwanted stock previously made for earlier scheduled orders. Production turned raw material into unwanted parts in order to 'clock up' its targeted overhead recoveries. Early cut-in dates of value engineered parts created out of specification stock. Parts made to forecast became unwanted stock when orders later failed to materialize.

- There was excessive waste, rework and duplication arising from process failures. As delivery dates drew near, pressure increased to ship part-finished assemblies so that invoices could be raised. Additional premium rate costs to finish assembly at the customer's location were then buried in the accounts.

The turning point came with the realization that inadequate cost information was the root cause of many of these problems. To understand the costs of process failure and to take a firm grip on product costs and profitability, the company embarked on an ABM project.

Using a multi-functional team, activity data from every department was collected and categorized into its basic 'core' activities – those that add value in some way – and 'diversionary' activities – those that merely dissipate value. Diversionary costs in the 'contract execution' process were high:

- 15 per cent caused by late programme changes
- 13 per cent from non-standard methods
- 18 per cent from process failures.

This gave a total of 46 per cent.

An understanding of these costs and their magnitude provided a vital focus for process improvement. When an ABM model of the business was built, real knowledge at last highlighted some solutions to the problems.

In the key process of responding to around 300 tender requests in a particular product/market segment, 230 were unsuccessful. A process cost of nearly £2m per annum of highly skilled engineers' estimating time included almost £500 000 of wasted effort! The ABM data provided superior product cost data in a form that gave rise to a simplified modular pricing mechanism. Not only did this save estimating time, it also provided an essential focus to only respond to those tender requests where the chances of winning were high.

In manufacturing, the cost rate per hour had included all the overheads recovered on direct hours. As the direct labour costs were only 10 per cent of total costs, this had created a serious distortion in the costing formula. In one machining cell, the setting time was 4 per cent of total production time, while the true costs were found to be 28 per cent of production costs. While Finance had been using a standard rate of £37 per hour, the real costs were found to be £28 for a production hour and £281 for a setting hour. With this knowledge, much closer attention was paid to the real relationship between production overheads, the causes of these overheads, and the products to which these overheads related. Discovering the real costs in production was a revelation, but the true benefit came when the cost base was reduced. ABM provided the focus to tackle the key high costs and their causes.

The distortion in product costing had also infected the calculations for capacity planning. All the previous numbers indicated that a high proportion of production had to go to sub-contractors at premium rates. In the production areas, people stood idle. The ABM results underlined something the unions had been pointing out for some time: the company was exporting jobs to other companies!

From the customer profitability analysis, a number of customer types were found to be at an uncomfortable level of profitability. Some customers were dropped, while a number of others were handled through a less costly channel. The overall sum of the margins now started to look healthier once nearly £1m of avoidable customer-related costs were eliminated. However, a major jump in profitability came when the root causes of diversionary activities were identified and the process improvements implemented. The additional capacity this provided allowed the increased volumes of profitable products sold to profitable customers to be processed at lower levels of unit costs. In the first year, the reduction in costs through reducing contractor premiums and the activities of handling contractors added another £1.5m to the bottom line.

The ABM analysis provided an insight into how the company could increase market share while at the same time creating a negative impact on its competitors. This was a case of using ABM to make a strategic strike at competitors.

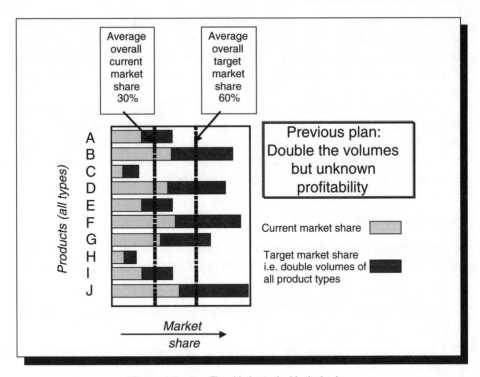

**Figure 10.18    The old plan to double the business**

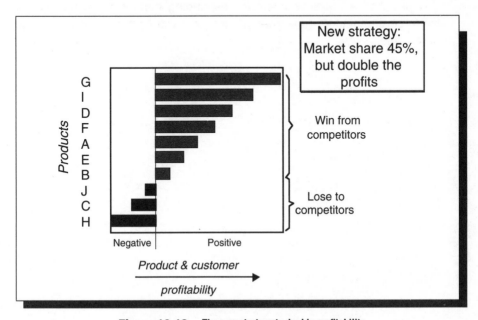

**Figure 10.19    The new strategy to double profitability**

The previous plan, as shown in Figure 10.18, was to increase market share across all the products to all the types of customer – in other words, just go for volume. With the knowledge from the ABM analysis, the company now knew the product and customer mixes where it did and did not want to win contracts, as shown in Figure 10.19.

However, by entering into a competitive tendering situation and forcing down the price, it knew exactly when to let a competitor win the bid, knowing that the competitor would now have an order that would be at a break-even or loss-making price. Had the company simply refused to bid, a competitor might have been left as the only contender, selling at a high price.

## LESSONS LEARNT

- ABM data, using attributes for the activities, provided a focus on process failures, the root cause of problems, and the route to process improvement.

- When the real costs were transparent, the company had the ability to balance the level of in-house manufacture and the use of sub-contractors properly.

- Accurate product costing and product profitability led to an improved product mix.

- ABM provided a strategic basis for expanding market share that would also force competitors (unknowingly) into winning contracts that would be unprofitable.

# A MERCHANTING COMPANY
## CUSTOMER PROFITABILITY ANALYSIS EXPOSED POOR PERFORMANCE MEASURES THAT WERE ERODING PROFITS

The merchanting company bought in a range of dry goods, and sold and distributed them to its customers via a regional warehouse network. In common with many businesses of this type, the company had built up a solid customer base offering a standard next-day delivery service to everyone. Although the gross margins from all customers were positive, the sector was experiencing pressures from its customers to reduce prices and improve levels of customer service. Management realized that existing management information offered limited support to the urgent commercial decisions they now faced.

However, under competitive pressure, management needed an accurate understanding of:

- the relationship between gross profit and trading profit, where trading profit equals gross profit minus selling, warehouse, distribution and stock-carrying costs
- volumes sold, stock policies and customer service levels.

To obtain a quick overall view of the business, the company decided to build a high-level ABM model before plunging into a lot of detailed analysis. This meant understanding the relationship between the major costs in the business and the key cost drivers. For the main activities, the first task was to determine their cost drivers.

The selling activity was made up from Central Office Sales, Regional Office Sales, the salesforce and Sales Administration. On investigation, the salesforce activity hardly ever involved prospecting for new business, but rather 'prompting' and collecting orders. Over 50 per cent of orders came via the Sales offices, which then reacted to the orders. On this basis, the key cost driver for all types of sales was taken as 'number of orders'. A weighting was applied to reflect some regional differences.

The majority of warehouse activity involved picking stock from pallet locations to make up orders. A small proportion of activity was consumed in putting away stock received from manufacturers. On this basis, the key cost driver for warehouse activity was taken as 'number of picks'. A 'pick' was an order line on a customer's order which represented a specific stock location in the warehouse. Customers were located around each regional warehouse. The mileage driven by each vehicle to the centre of its delivery round was small. On this basis, the key cost driver was taken as 'number of drops'. A 'drop' was a stop at a customer to offload an order. The total warehouse stocking cost (cash tied up in inventory) was calculated on the basis that the value of stock per tonne was very similar across all product lines. On this basis, the key cost driver was taken as 'number of tonnes delivered'.

From the company's normal transaction data in the system for each month, and cumulatively throughout the year, the total of each type of cost and the cost driver volumes were found. From this data and the cost driver volumes, the unit costs were calculated. For example, total delivery costs were £221 000, and a total of 18 700 drops at customers were made, so the unit cost per drop was £11.78. For each customer over the same period, the revenue, purchase costs, number of drops, picks, tonnes and orders were found from the management information system. Costs were assigned to customers by multiplying actual cost driver volumes for each customer by the unit costs calculated from the total throughputs in the analysis period. One customer, for example, had 12 delivery drops, so the delivery costs were that number of drops multiplied by the unit costs (12 times £11.78).

Trading profit (gross profit minus selling, warehouse, distribution and stock-carrying costs) for each customer was then used to plot a hook curve of cumulative trading profit, from highest through to lowest, as shown in Figure 10.20.

The hook curve gave the first indications of where the company could start to offer differentiated service levels. The potential 'Gold' customers would be the 30 per cent that provided 80 per cent of the trading profit. The 'Silver' customers would be those that provided the next 20 per cent of trading profit. The last 20 per cent were showing a negative trading profit, and unless there was good reason to keep them, they became candidates for elimination or being kept at a service level that reduced costs.

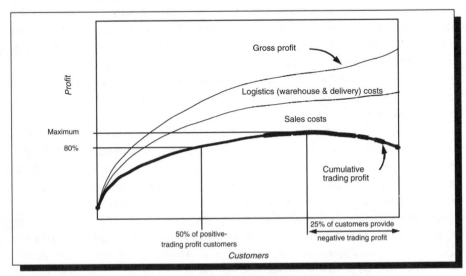

**Figure 10.20**   Cumulative trading and gross profit

However, when the sales and logistics costs were added to the trading profit for each company in the sequence, the gross profit curve that appeared had an odd characteristic. It seemed that some of the sales attracted a high gross profit, but the costs of servicing the account severely eroded this figure. This prompted the company to extend the analysis to try to uncover the root causes. Many customers taking small volumes provided a negative trading profit as a percentage of sales revenue. These became candidates either for elimination, or a change in relationship, such as higher prices for the service level. More seriously, a significant number of customers were also negative, but took a high volume of products. With discount pressure, the company had to look seriously at costs. At this point the analysis turned to 'data tunnelling', a technique whereby you plot variables against each other to look for curious or significant relationships. A number of these were found.

The number of picks in the warehouse was a key cost driver. A number of customers had a disproportionately high number of picks for the volumes they ordered. Each of these customers' trading relationships with the company had to be scrutinized to determine whether there was likely to be a trend in the future towards higher volumes per order line which would reduce the impact of the warehouse activity on the costs of servicing the customer. Given the high costs of the sales activities, a graph was plotted of the sales cost against the volume the customers ordered in a given period. The sales costs for one segment of customers were very high, given that the volume that resulted from the sales activities was small. Why were there so many customers that seemed to require such a high level of sales activity for such a poor result? For many customers, the high sales costs led to the negative trading profit. Unusually, many of the sales to this segment of customers had some of the highest gross profits.

The overall proportions of overhead costs indicated that inventory costs (cash tied up in stock in the warehouses) was unusually high for this type of merchanting business. This confirmed the need to analyse stock policies and demand patterns. The cumulative volume curve, based on starting with the highest-demand product line, showed that out of total of 1372 lines stocked, 88 accounted for 50 per cent of the demand, 613 accounted for 45 per cent, and the remaining 671 lines only accounted for the final 5 per cent of demand. This is a characteristic of nearly every warehouse anywhere. There is always a tail of slow-moving stock where you can find pallets of goods with thick layers of dust on them.

To complete the analysis, the amount of stock held for the product lines was also investigated. Overall, the company was achieving a stock turn of 9. From the analysis, stock turns were found to be 24 for fast-moving lines, 8 for medium and 1.4 for slow. However, Head Office was putting pressure on the Merchanting division to improve this figure. How was such pressure usually met? The simplest and quickest route was to stop ordering fast-moving lines so the warehouses drained of stock. Stock turns improved, but at the expense of more frequent stock-outs. This situation continued until customer complaints to the Chief Executive forced more stock back into the system. The impact of holding stock of the medium- and slow-moving lines was also seen in inventory costs. Medium lines had enough sales history to be statistically susceptible to using modern forecasting techniques. Stock control in the past had been largely a rule-of-thumb exercise.

Stocks of slow-moving lines were caused by a number of factors:

- failed launches of products, with the residue left in stock
- special service arrangements made by salespeople for particular customers
- minimum order quantities set by the manufacturers.

For these lines, serious consideration had to be given to sourcing them from other specialist merchants. Also, a thorough purge of the slow-moving lines had to be undertaken by every region. These actions significantly reduced inventory costs.

But why had such high warehouse and logistics costs grown over the years, despite constant management attention to keep the trend in check? Finally, the root cause was uncovered. Traditionally, the salesforce had been paid a bonus based on gross profit. As a result, adding additional lines to stock, or incurring extra costs for small orders or tortuous and expensive special deliveries, had no impact on their bonus. On the contrary, they would do many things, at any expense, to achieve a high gross-profit sale. The ABM analysis had been fundamental in uncovering the major issue: bonuses to the salesforce. A change to paying bonuses based on trading profit had an overnight impact on the salesforce's behaviour, and led to a change to all customers becoming positive in terms of trading profit. The refined analysis of trading profit re-segmented the customers into the Gold, Silver and Bronze categories.

More detailed analysis uncovered the potential for changing the service levels offered to customers. Among the Gold customers, research had indicated that a 'same-day' delivery service would increase market share. The ABM data was used to model various scenarios in terms of order cut-off times, volume throughputs in relation to vehicle size, and utilization throughout the day. The key was to maximize the use of the assets, both vehicles and the people working in the logistics chain. Other customers in the Silver category were generally happy to receive the traditional next-day service. Those in the Bronze category were either candidates for next-day service, or longer intervals of supply essentially determined by efficient delivery route planning.

The ABM techniques reduced unit costs and improved customer service levels profitably. It was acknowledged that ABM had provided a superior result compared to the conventional techniques that had been used in the past to resolve logistics problems.

## LESSONS LEARNT

- A high-level ABM model can give many preliminary insights that focus on where root causes of problems lie.

- Data tunnelling (or data mining) is a useful technique to extract further subtle relationships from the ABM analysis data.

- When things start to look very odd in companies, look at the measures being used. Behaviours – particularly many of the strangest ones – will be determined by the measures.

- The ABM model is an ideal source of data for creating various scenarios of alternative operating strategies.

# A GLOBAL MANUFACTURER AND SUPPLIER OF ORTHOPAEDIC IMPLANTS AND SURGICAL INSTRUMENTATION
## WHEN THE PROFITABLE SEGMENTS ARE FOUND, ENHANCING SERVICE LEVELS HELPS TO RETAIN CUSTOMERS

The company had manufacturing plants in two European countries, with sales via a single European distribution centre.

Following the ABM analysis, the company was heartened to discover that nearly all of its customers, mainly hospitals and clinics, were making a positive contribution. At the product level, every product made a positive contribution. They were anxious, however, to maintain their profitability despite the continuing erosion of gross margins in their longer-established products, and their competitors' apparent willingness to provide a superior service to their own customers at no extra cost. They therefore needed to understand the cost implications of matching their competitors' actions, and to find the most favourable product ranges in which to focus future development. Their product portfolio contained over 1300 appliances and instruments. Some product ranges were based on the latest available materials and surgical know-how, but there existed a long tail of small-batch items, mainly based on older, superseded technology. The ABM cumulative product group profitability is shown in Figure 10.21.

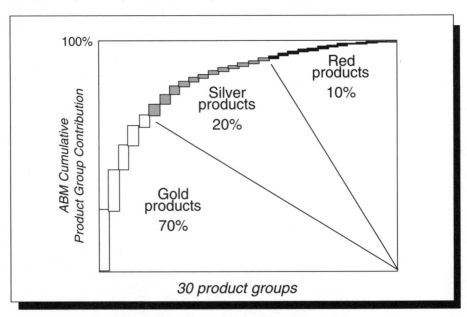

**Figure 10.21**   Cumulative product group profitability

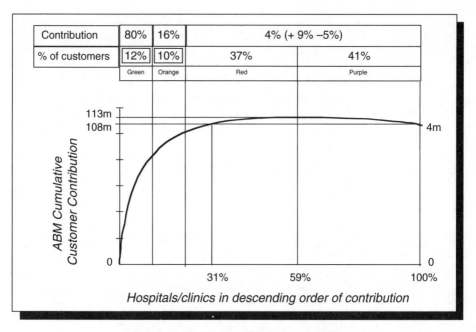

**Figure 10.22** Cumulative customer contribution

The activity-based costs of all the mainstream products were significantly lower than previously thought, while those of the tail products were generally slightly higher. Based on the analysis, the product groups were categorized into Gold, Silver or Red, according to their ABM profitability. The analysis of ABM Cumulative Customer Contribution is shown in Figure 10.22. Based on contribution the customers were categorized as Green, Orange, Red or Purple.

Because customer-driven costs were relatively low, customer profitability correlated very closely with the products that they bought. Green customers bought predominantly Gold products, Orange customers bought similar quantities of Gold, Silver and Red products, while Red and Purple customers bought mainly the tail of Red products. The previous custom and practice for the salesforce was to share their time across customers, in many cases biasing their sales time towards the higher-volume customers. The ABM analysis showed that the single highest-contributing customer out of a customer base of 1305 gave a contribution equal to the sum of the contributions of the tail of 1005 customers. Losing any of the highest-contributing customers would have created a desperate position for the company. This was the first alert to management that it needed to change the use of the salesforce's time.

From a product perspective, the implication for the selling strategy seemed simple: focus on new, high-margin products. This was complicated by the

| Currently profitable | Potentially profitable | Previously profitable | Unprofitable |
|---|---|---|---|
| Established<br><br>Top products dominate<br><br>Strong relationship | New customer<br><br>Just profitable<br><br>Product tail dominates – investment?<br><br>Surgeons are opinion-formers<br><br>Building relationship | Was profitable<br><br>Now unprofitable<br><br>Lost top products – tail dominates<br><br>Potential return to profitability | Unprofitable<br><br>No likelihood of buying top products<br><br>Resource diversion<br><br>Limited or no medium/long-term potential |
| Explore new opportunities to develop the relationship | Invest, with focus on top products<br><br>Build relationship and service | Assess potential for top products<br><br>Rebuild relationship? | Refocus resources |

**Figure 10.23** The new salesforce strategy

preferences of different customer groups. One reported risk was that newer products lacked the decades of clinical history which surgeons were said to insist upon. But in other cases, some surgeons were keen to fit the latest implants to patients and to participate in product development. The clear message was that it was vital to understand customer needs and preferences clearly on an individual basis.

Tail products, though low in contribution terms, were nevertheless important, according to the salesforce, because many customers would only buy from a 'one-stop shop' that stocked a complete range. Some of the tail products also had a valuable role as a low-cost, low-risk introduction route for new customers.

The strategy for Red customers therefore depended on their potential for becoming advocates in the longer term, while the loyalty of Gold and Silver customers had to be nurtured and developed. An overall strategy for the sales-force was developed, as shown in Figure 10.23.

The ABM analysis also threw up a counter-intuitive result. Most customers' demands, as it transpired, drove far less cost than was thought. This revelation changed management's whole view of the role of the salesforce. For example, 'in-theatre' training on the use of the products, in the past seen as a distraction for the salesforce, now came to be viewed as a core service. Customers who had previously been perceived as abusing this service by using salespeople as unpaid ancillary staff were in the main perfectly willing to pay a reasonable charge. This led to the formation of a team of dedicated theatre support staff, an action that created further advocacy and, importantly, was the main factor in locking out competitors.

Confident in the outcome from the ABM analysis so far, the company then turned its attention to the global picture. Here lay the greatest paradox. Products were manufactured in many locations around the world, and passed through a regional, then a national warehouse *en route* to the customer. Yet the most profitable customer lay within a stone's throw of the factory making the most profitable products. This finding led to a root-and-branch review of the objectives, the performance and indeed the relevance of the global distribution system. The ABM team sharpened their pencils and set to on what was to become the project with the greatest positive impact on corporate results that the company had ever known.

Now that senior management was free from the relentless pressure to cut costs arbitrarily, it found time to consider innovative ideas to ensure the success of the business in the longer term. Management used ABM to model new scenarios so that it could consider manufacturing implants to order, and delivering them just in time. It proposed to provide instrumentation that would be specific to the patient need, maintain a worldwide centre of excellence in reconstructive orthopaedic surgery, and provide advanced in-theatre expert advice – personally, or remotely by video link and the Internet. With the help of technology, it also proposed to maintain a database of clinical history – 'knowledge management' on behalf of its customers.

## LESSONS LEARNT

- Segmenting products and customers in terms of profitability, then linking the two together provided a rational basis to change the sales strategy.

- The activity data on the customer relationships, coupled with the dialogue with customers, exposed a completely new customer relationship opportunity that helped to build higher levels of trust and customer loyalty.

- The basis for continuing with the same global distribution system was challenged by exposing the current unnecessary costs of the current method.

- Managers freed from chasing the wrong issues were able to devote core time to growing the business profitably.

# A SPECIALIST DISTRIBUTION COMPANY
## UNCOVERING THE COMPLEXITY OF HAVING MANY SUPPLIERS OF MANY PRODUCTS GOING TO MANY CUSTOMERS

The new owners of a specialist distributor provided a tough challenge to the management team – improve returns on capital from a meagre 6 per cent to 18 per cent, equivalent to a trebling of profits!

The company faced other challenges. Retailers were seeking bigger discounts, better stock availability and more technical support. Robust competition was forcing the business to work very hard just to hold on to its retail channels. Suppliers insisted that the business stocked and distributed a very broad product range, from items costing a few pence to thousands of pounds. The business operated several warehouses located around the country. Only its largest suppliers delivered products to all warehouses. The smaller suppliers delivered to the most convenient warehouse for them, and the business balanced its inventory by moving stock around the warehouses.

The turning point came when an activity-based analysis revealed the true cost of balancing inventory around the warehouses. For every £1 the company spent on the activities of purchasing, paying suppliers, receiving and storing incoming goods, it spent a further 41p on moving stock from warehouse to warehouse. Despite the balancing process, it was still frequently necessary to express deliver goods to customers at the other end of the country, at further cost. The breakdown of costs is shown in Figure 10.24.

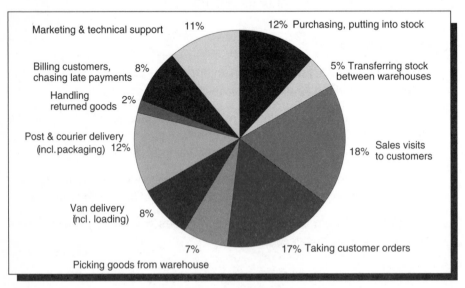

**Figure 10.24**   Breakdown of logistics costs

Within three months, the company had plans in place to carry all their stock in a single warehouse. This, plus other improvements, allowed the business to reduce overheads by over a third, while actually improving availability and speed of delivery to customers. Moving to a single warehouse structure naturally forced a major rethink of logistics. The old warehouse locations enabled the company's own delivery vehicles to make round trips covering 20 or so retailers in a day. As well as providing the 'personal touch', this method has been frequently benchmarked against contract hauliers and courier companies, and found to be more cost-effective. Couriers continued to be used to reach more distant retail customers. How would this change the business, what were the cost implications, and how would customers react?

For many customers, nothing has changed. Improvements in the motorway network have brought many new retailer locations within the 'one-day radius' of the surviving warehouse. A further band can be reached through a relay technique: early every morning, a driver from the warehouse hands over a full vehicle to a local driver and drives yesterday's empty one back. The cost impact of switching the more distant customers from own-fleet to courier delivery has largely been offset by the reduction in emergency shipments, most of which were sent by courier in the past. The salesforce continues to have national coverage, though most are now based at home rather than the nearest warehouse. The typical agenda of a customer call has changed somewhat, from chasing (and often delivering) late consignments to stock planning for new products and the new season.

As well as eliminating the need to transfer stock between warehouses, the restructuring had a significant impact on several other activities, as depicted by the black bars in Figure 10.25. The grey bars show the potential for further cost savings where diversionary activity had been identified by the staff themselves. Dealing with late deliveries during sales visits to customers proved to be the most significant. In this case, management chose not to reduce the sales team by 50 per cent, but instead to set new sales-related priorities for the additional time now made available.

Returned goods were another drain on people's time. Prior to the activity analysis, it was known that around 20 per cent of order items were returned, and this was generally assumed to be the norm in this specialist sector, given the technical nature of the products. When the cost of handling returns was found to match or often exceed the value of the goods handled, there was a clear need to understand why goods were returned. The principal cause proved not to be product failure, but customer behaviour – some large retailers were deliberately over-ordering. Months or years later, they would successfully claim a full refund for out-of-date stock. In turn there were two main causes for over-ordering:

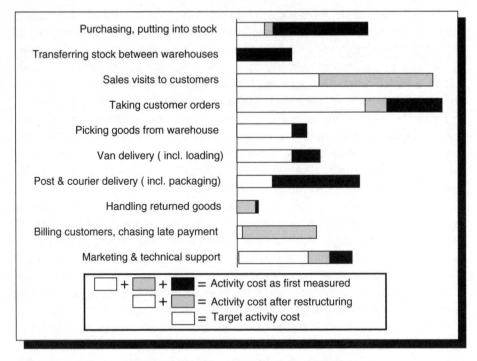

**Figure 10.25**   The potential for further cost savings

- unreliable supply
- sales promotions by the distributor to encourage retailers to buy in stock – unfortunately, these were not complemented with promotions to end-customers.

Both of these causes could now be addressed by the distributor, without the need to 'take a stick' to errant retailers.

However, it was also believed that some retailers were over-ordering specu-latively when they heard rumours of impending shortages and price rises, or at the end of a sales promotion. Goods bought at a lower price could later attract a higher refund. This was effectively eliminated by a new bar-coding system intro-duced in the sole warehouse. The business had hundreds of suppliers, but half of them eroded profits by 7 per cent while only generating 3 per cent of total sales. Handling small parts and spares created the greatest losses. Not only did these carry high handling costs for negligible margins, but frequent shortages also generated additional diversionary costs as the business chased back-orders to meet customer demand. Eliminating unprofitable suppliers could in theory reduce inventories by 10 per cent and overheads by over 3 per cent.

However, there were also options for turning unprofitable supplier relationships around. Supplier profitability was actually improved in a variety of ways:

- The lowest-volume suppliers were simply 'rationalized out', especially where they competed with another supplier.
- Some suppliers are now financing additional stock levels of low-value and spare parts. In effect, the distributor's warehouse becomes an extension of the suppliers' finished goods stores. Both parties save through a reduction in panic orders.
- Some suppliers of low-cost, high-margin goods have agreed to reimburse for unsold goods, taking the lead from the newspaper industry. The distributor and retailers can now carry higher stocks without financial risk, and all parties are sharing the benefits of higher sales volumes.

The improvement in return on capital employed was achieved not only through improving profits, but also through reducing the capital employed, much of which was tied up in inventories. Overall, the stock turned over three times per year; 45 per cent of products, representing only 10 per cent of sales, turned over at half this rate or less. Yet 12 per cent of product lines, representing 5 per cent of sales, were out of stock at all warehouses.

Amalgamating the warehouse stocks has reduced the effect of random variability of demand, and thus the need to keep such high inventory levels. However, the greater part of the saving has been through closer monitoring of demand patterns and suppliers' plans for updated designs, so that stocks of obsolescent lines are now run down earlier without the need for heavy discounting. Amalgamating warehouses has also eliminated one major cause of stockouts: the sheer complexity of the ordering algorithm. The other principal issue has been the failure of some suppliers to meet their own delivery lead times: this is now being addressed with the most persistent offenders.

Some of the more complex, higher-margin products proved to be less profitable than expected due to failure in service, even when caused by end-customer misuse. This resulted in activities such as claim-handling, obtaining and supplying warranty spares, unpaid servicing and repairs, fault investigation and communication to reassure the end-customer community. Knowledge of these costs motivated the company to engage in robust discussions with certain suppliers with the aim of eliminating all potential causes of such failures.

A year later, the company was quick to acknowledge that the ABM analysis had led to savings of one-third of overheads through warehouse and supplier rationalization. Higher availability and quicker customer response led to greater customer loyalty, and a new partnership relationship with suppliers and customers.

## LESSONS LEARNT

- Activity-based analysis revealed the true cost of balancing inventory around the warehouses, and provided the proof to support a warehouse rationalization programme.

- The data enabled a proper evaluation to be undertaken to judge the optimum level of in-house and contractor delivery services.

- Customer behaviours were exposed as a major root cause of unnecessary costs.

- The ABM analysis provided the basis for determining options for turning round unprofitable supplier relationships.

- Above all, the study showed that players in the middle of a supply chain do not have to regard themselves as squeezed from both sides – they just have more parties with whom to negotiate. Success in this field depends critically on being well informed.

# AN ADVERTISING DIRECTORY COMPANY
## BETTER INFORMATION TO SUPPORT PRODUCT COSTING, CUSTOMER PROFITABILITY, BENCHMARKING AND PROCESS IMPROVEMENT

The company produced directories of adverts for services categorized by type of service. The directories were reprinted annually. One range of products went to every household in the country; another product went to every business. Although every business with a telephone number received a free single-line entry in the directory, the revenue to the business came from selling a larger advert, ranging from a lowly single-line entry in bold type through to full-page display advertisements. To cover the whole country, over 80 different directories were printed. Some customers (advertisers) would have entries in all the directories, to ensure national coverage.

In the printed directories, customers paid for the design and set-up for the advert, and then a price based on the area of the page occupied by the advert. The 'cost' of searching for a particular service in the directory was borne by the user of the service; they simply picked up the directory at home or at work and looked through it for a supplier of the service they needed. The costs of selling adverts, preparing them for printing, printing the directories and distributing them to households and businesses had to be covered by the revenue from the advertisers.

A third product was an equivalent service via a toll-free telephone number. Here the cost structure is different. Advertisers pay to have their name listed for selection should a user of the service be looking for a supplier in their category. When a user telephones the service, the cost of the search is borne by the company. In this case, there is a risk that a very popular service, such as 'What's on at the cinema', will attract many callers, but the charge to the customer for being listed is far less than the cost of the toll-free calls.

The company was keen to understand the dynamics of the business for all its products, and in particular it wanted to have much higher visibility of the costs to service each product so that it could remove the effects of cross-subsidization that distorted the product profitability reported in the accounts. Its ABM model had to answer a number of fundamental questions:

- What is the activity-based cost of the products, channels to market, and specific customer segments?
- What drives the costs?
- What is our profitability profile of products and customers?
- Is there a break-point in our process costs for multiple sales that would support a discount structure for larger customers?

- What are the costs of our processes in terms of core and diversionary (the costs of process failures)?
- What process improvement opportunities exist, and what are they worth?

The scope included all Head Office functions, Regional Offices and the whole Sales network: a total of over 2900 staff. Including the direct product costs, the scope was over £260 million.

The ABM model was designed to provide a cascade of cost objects – first, the key products, then by region (individual directory), then by type of advert, then by size within type. This created over 1000 cost objects. Customers were segmented by their service or product code (where they featured in the directory) and by using attributes, further segmented into other characteristics such as payment history.

The starting point for the model – the resources – held over 250 ledger lines used to define budgets and actuals in each of the 17 functions. Activity data for every department was collected, and the costs from the ledger assigned to activities using appropriate resource drivers. Support departments and activities were reassigned to the frontline activities, which in turn were assigned to all the cost objects.

The first major result from the ABM analysis was a change in the amount that could now be considered a direct cost rather than an overhead. Over 13 per cent of the total costs changed between the two categories. Direct costs increased by 21 per cent, and overheads reduced by 35 per cent. The remaining overheads fell into the ABM categories of infrastructure and sustaining, amounting to a total of 25 per cent of total costs. In the accounts, overheads had previously been assumed to be nearly 40 per cent of total costs.

The next key result was the cost of producing each regional and area directory: three out of over 80 different directories are shown in Figure 10.26. In a business zone, many advertisers would be featured, many with large advertisements. In the same area, there would be many households, each receiving a directory. These two aspects created high production costs. In a rural area, the proportion of sales costs predominated. The salesforce had to cover a large distance between customers. Production costs were low, as the area contained a sparse population. In an inner-city area, sales costs were low as there was a high density of customers, so the salesforce could visit many customers in a day. However, there was a marked difference in the 'quality' of many inner-city customers, many of them becoming difficult payers or just ending up as bad debts.

The analysis of every process had to identify all the activity steps involved in making a large number of combinations of sales, and the preparation and productions costs for those customers who ordered more than one advert in one directory. This analysis was focused on searching for any significant cost break-

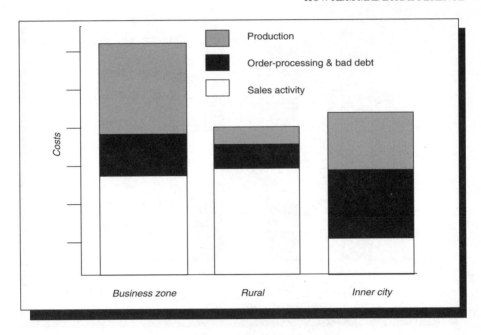

**Figure 10.26** Cost to produce directories

points that could allow the company to offer discounts that reflected the reduced processing costs.

The whole sales process was a standardized method across the whole country. The ABM data from every region showed that each process step was featured, but the proportions of each varied, as did the final revenue-to-total-cost ratio, as shown in Figure 10.27, which compares three of the regions. This type of data was ideal for benchmarking and searching for best practice. Small percentage changes to the revenue/cost ratio had a major positive impact on corporate profitability.

When assigning activities to products, an interesting dilemma faced the company. The activities of planning the sales visits were associated with a customer, as was travelling to the location. All the costs of unsuccessful sales visits also fell into this category. The selling activity itself was associated with the product being sold, as was any subsequent paperwork to load the customer's order on to the system. The key question then arose concerning how to assign any of the 'sales overheads' costs that could not be directly traced to a product. The company had a number of options:

● The first option was to assign the sales overhead costs based on the time spent attempting to sell all three products. This was the portfolio approach, on the basis that the purpose of the visit was to sell all three products.

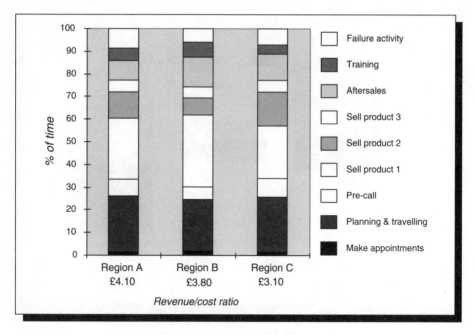

**Figure 10.27** Benchmarking and searching for best practice

- The second option was to assign all sales overheads to the primary product. This is the marginal approach, but only the direct selling costs would then be assigned to other products. The primary product would be subsidizing the other products.

- The third option was to assign all the costs based on which products were sold, irrespective of the actual selling effort on any of the products. From a modelling perspective, the third option was easy to link to sales history files, but there was no viable financial logic to this approach.

Whether to go for the portfolio approach or the marginal approach is always a matter of choice, based on what the model has been constructed to achieve. However, whatever route is taken must be clearly stated so that everyone interprets the outcome of the ABM analysis in the same manner. In this company's case, the portfolio approach was used to create a visible split between all the products, on the basis that profitability should be shown with a minimum of cross-subsidization.

The ABM database provided unit cost data that was invaluable in focusing attention on process failures and the costs of handling various customer behaviours. An example of the data is shown in Figure 10.28.

One important use of the unit cost data was the introduction of Activity Based

194

| Activity | Total cost | Cost driver | Volume | Unit cost |
|---|---|---|---|---|
| Handling sales enquiries | £59 634 | No. of sales enquiries | 3400 | £17.54 |
| Amendments to orders | £27 451 | No. of amendments | 9170 | £12.91 |
| Complaint visits to customer | £61 962 | No. of visits | 150 | £413.08 |
| Credit checking | £56 059 | No. of new accounts | 9200 | £6.09 |

**Figure 10.28**    Unit costs focus on process failures and customer behaviours

Budgeting. Managers forecast the cost driver volumes, which are then related back through the activities to determine the resources required.

The ABM model proved to be a major asset for the company in terms of prompting major productivity improvements in all processes. With the advent of the Internet, the model found a new role in simulating new products and routes to market. Using ABM eliminated much of the previous guesswork and uncertainty about new initiatives.

## LESSONS LEARNT

● ABM activity analysis created the necessary transparency of costs to make a clear separation between businesses split on a product basis.

● Comparative data for benchmarking brought to light areas of best practice to be used across the whole business.

● In an ABM model, many costs can be assigned in a number of ways. The chosen method will be an assumption for that model only. Further models can be constructed for comparison based on changing these assumptions. To avoid wrong conclusions being drawn from the outputs from the model, it is imperative that these assumptions are recorded and reported along with the model outputs.

# A HIGH STREET RETAILING COMPANY
## SUBTLE CHANGES CAN MAKE DRAMATIC IMPROVEMENTS

A European franchisee of a renowned high street store chain had run its local three-store operation profitably for many years. Although sales volumes were growing, it was nevertheless experiencing a steady decline in profits. Because of its location outside the UK, products were delivered directly from the franchise owner along a ten-day supply chain, thus requiring a local warehouse. A further constraint was a tight labour market – the stores were unable to fill current vacancies, let alone expand the labour force.

The franchise offered products to the franchise stores at a fixed sales price and margin, the latter varying only slightly between product ranges. As a result, all products appeared equally profitable when conventionally accounted for. Managers knew this could not be right – with product ranges including specialist foods, gifts and textiles, warehousing and overhead costs could not be allocated neatly according to margin per square metre. A system whereby the true costs of stocking individual products was found had to be the key to discovering the most profitable mix of products. The business needed a method that would allow it to predict the impact on profit and resources of changes to the product mix in each of the stores.

An ABM project was set up, as a result of which the franchise was able to:

- increase revenue by 11 per cent and profit by 44 per cent within three months
- increase sales volume by 8 per cent, while reducing staff numbers by 6 per cent.

The project began by identifying the key business processes in the franchise operation, breaking these down into activities, and then identifying the costs of activities and the frequency with which they were carried out, by product. An occupation charge was calculated to represent the cost of storage, both in the franchisee's warehouse and in the stores. For some of the slower-moving low-value products, the cost of providing floor space approached 20 per cent of the revenue generated. In contrast, for some faster-moving products it was as low as 1 per cent of revenue. For the very slow-moving products, this issue alone dominated the profit equation. The profit per square metre is shown in Figure 10.29.

However, product stock-turn was not the only element that could have a dramatic impact on profitability. The second most profitable product range, when judged by the margin generated per square metre was stationery and gifts. Yet it proved to be unprofitable when analysed using ABM. The product actually cost 2 per cent more to sell through the store than the revenue it

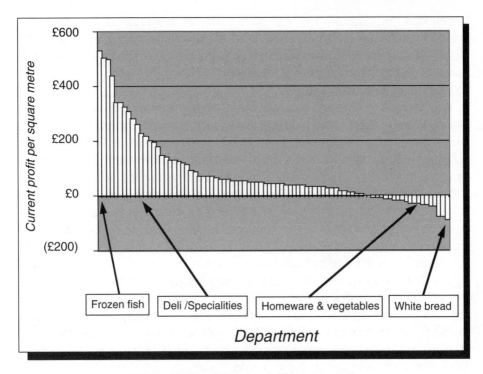

**Figure 10.29**   Retail store profit per square metre

generated. The immediate reaction was to discontinue the range and use the floor space for something more profitable, but a more considered reaction was to find out whether profitability could be improved.

The franchise owner allowed the franchisee around 30 per cent margin on all items of stationery and gifts sold. In addition to the cost of sales, the costs of credit card handling, discounts, merchandising and overhead costs were assigned on the basis of the actual amount of resources consumed by each product. The make-up of costs for the stationery and gift products as a percentage of revenue found that 70 per cent was the cost of sales, the balance being made up from 8 per cent to process the item through the till, 6 per cent for shop floor space, 6 per cent to merchandise the product and the rest from ordering, delivery and customer service.

At 6 per cent of revenue, the cost of merchandising stationery and gifts seemed extremely high as a proportion of revenue. For the majority of other product ranges, this was less than 1 per cent. Digging deeper into the statistics found the cause. Gifts and stationery comprised the fourth largest range of products in the store, but were only the thirty-sixth highest in terms of turnover. Merchandising costs, such as refilling the shelves and bringing stock in from the warehouse, quickly eroded the profitability of low-price items. However, although stationery and gifts generated good volume throughputs and floor space was well planned, they were finally acknowledged to be no longer a viable range for the store on account of their low profitability. The space was assigned to promote other product ranges.

Another type of ABM analysis, unit costs, did highlight where savings could be made. The unit costs of the food and textile cash tills were compared. Unit costs of the food tills were 5p, and those of the textiles tills were 24p. There was roughly the same number of tills, but for food products they were all in one bank, and hence the capacity was easier to manage. The textiles' tills were in eight banks, all of which are staffed all of the time. Unfortunately, there was no way to remove all the spare capacity in the tills as they were split between four locations. However, by reducing the number of banks to five, spare capacity at off-peak times was reduced by 60 per cent and the unit cost of a textile till transaction was reduced by more than 30 per cent.

The ABM analysis also focused on processes. Each Friday, the local warehouse had to contend with both the arrival of a container from the UK and picking for the stores. However, 45 per cent of orders on a Friday were for non-core products. As a result, some core products were not picked in time for the busiest trading day. This simple failure was estimated to cost the business £700 000 in lost sales per annum for one product category alone!

Examining the size of orders, it was found that a large amount of effort went into fulfilling small orders. For example, over 50 per cent of orders for lingerie separates were for single items, even though lingerie separates were a major product line with a high turnover of product, and ample shelf space. This finding called into question the store's policy of keeping the shelves as full as possible at all times. Some minor process changes brought an immediate improvement in:

- minimum order quantities across a range of products
- prioritizing order checks in the store
- increased computerization of the process.

Together, these measures reduced the average cost of moving a product from the warehouse to the store by a third, and the effort involved by 45 per cent. It also ensured that the warehouse was able to meet all Friday orders for core products, adding £2m a year in sales that would otherwise have been lost.

The ABM model enabled store management to model the effects on the delicate balance of profitability, occupation and resources of any change in product mix and floor space.

Figure 10.30 shows the final strategy for one of the stores. Each pair of circles represents a different range of products. The vertical axis measures the amount

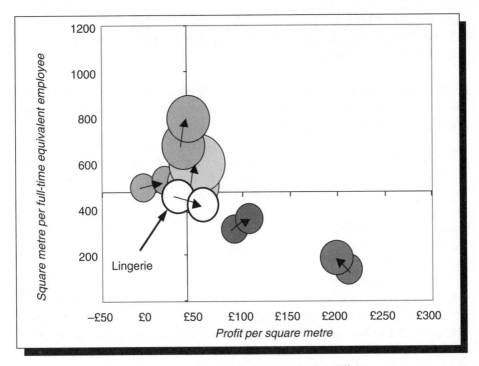

**Figure 10.30**   Planning a new strategy for the retail store

of effort per square metre that the range will require. The horizontal axis shows contribution per square metre. The size of the bubble indicates the floor space allocated to the product range. The arrow indicates the direction of change as a result of the new strategy. In the diagram, the white bubbles show the impact of the new strategy on the lingerie product group. Sales volumes rose by 100 per cent as a result of providing more floor space and improving product availability on key trading days. ABM provided the managers of the franchise stores with a powerful tool to assist decision-making.

## LESSONS LEARNT

- In a retail business, using gross margin as an indicator of profitability can be very unwise. The actual costs throughout the business, when assigned to each product, create the true contribution that each product is generating. There will be surprising and unexpected differences.

- Management discovered that relatively subtle changes to processes and product mix can have a dramatic impact on the bottom line.

# AN ELECTRICITY SUPPLY COMPANY
## UNCOVERING THE TRUE IMPACT ON PROFITABILITY OF THE BEHAVIOUR OF MILLIONS OF CUSTOMERS

The company faced a gradual decline in its domestic customer base, despite intense activity to develop new products and services. It was also under severe pressure from its main shareholder to improve profitability.

The Directors considered a percentage reduction in staff across the business, but they realized that this would only create problems in the future. The same levels of customer service would still have to be achieved, but with fewer people. The risk of reducing service levels was not one they wished to contemplate when there was already a net outflow of customers. Two ways forward presented themselves: improving processes to reduce waste and duplication, and looking very carefully at unprofitable domestic customers. An ABM study was launched with these objectives.

Within four months, the business identified the groups of customers eroding the greatest profit, and proposed new processes to restore them to profitability. Taken together, these changes added almost £8m a year to the bottom line. Managers also proposed a move away from traditional budgeting practices towards a system of rolling forecasts based on the key drivers of costs within the business. This would allow resource planning to be much more responsive to changes in the marketplace and eliminate much of the time-consuming annual

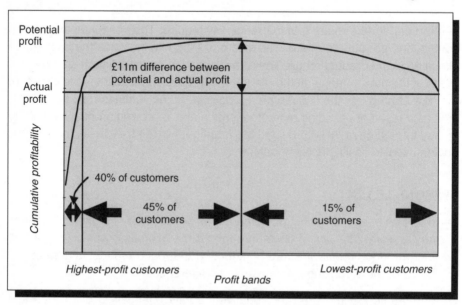

**Figure 10.31**   Cumulative profitability of domestic customers

haggling over resources. The fact that some domestic customers were unprofitable was no surprise. But the actual number became the turning point in the study: 5 per cent was anticipated, but the ABM model found the real proportion to be over 15 per cent, reducing the profitability of the business by £11m a year. This meant that the total profit made from 60 per cent of domestic customers was zero, as shown in Figure 10.31.

This raised a number of fundamental questions:

- Which domestic customers should they focus on retaining?
- Could previously unprofitable customers be restored to profit?
- If customers could not be made profitable, would the business be happy to see them go?
- On which groups should customer acquisition be focused?

The analyses provided some sobering surprises. For example, the unprofitable group included many who paid by standing order or direct debit, traditionally the mark of a valued customer. It was surprising how quickly a number of small activities could accumulate and erode profitability to zero even for a valued customer, as shown in Figure 10.32.

The total cost of a customer who ran the full gauntlet of debt prevention and recovery activities exceeded the average gross margin per quarter for a domestic customer by almost 600 per cent. In other words, at best, no profit

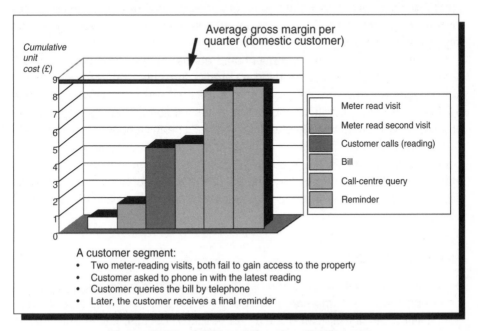

**Figure 10.32**   Activities quickly erode profitability to zero

could be made from them for another six quarters. Thankfully, the number of customers experiencing the full range of activities was limited. About 10 per cent of all customers were visited every year to address the issue of mounting debt – and the business would have done more had the resources been available. However, less than 40 per cent of those eventually had warrants issued against them to permit entry to premises for the fitting of pre-payment meters. This drove home to managers the importance of predicting debt as early as possible to avoid the need for all the expensive follow-on activities.

The balance of activities has shifted to the front end of the process. Credit vetting has been improved. Innovative but restrictive payment options are offered to new customers and those seeking to move away from pre-payment meters. Verbal communication now begins well in advance of the issue of a statutory warning of disconnection. As a result, debt recovery visits and warrants served – by far the most costly of the back-end activities – have so far fallen by 30 per cent. Many customers remain profitable who would otherwise have cost the business money.

A further 12 profit-eroding issues were identified. Each was the focus for cross-functional meetings of managers, during which root causes were thrashed out and proposals for improvement developed. Fifteen key proposals for change were raised, 12 of which were implemented in the course of the following year. Each helped to lift a number of loss-making customers back into profit and raise profitability across all groups of customers. In total, they delivered an additional £8m to the bottom line. Each proposal represents both a cost saving and an improvement in service to the customer.

Prior to the ABM study, a conventional annual budget process was used. Now, the ABM model can be used to predict the effect that changes in the marketplace will have on resources across the business. The business still has a budget process, but it has become a less time-consuming and divisive process, and it is beginning to question whether it needs a budget process at all.

The business now has plans in place that that will satisfy its major shareholder's expectations. More importantly, in terms of the proposals planned and managers' enthusiasm for embedding the use of ABM techniques, the business has made great strides in providing excellent customer service at the lowest cost.

## LESSONS LEARNT

- In businesses with a large number of customers and a low average margin per customer, it is imperative to uncover the true causes and level of profitability at as fine a level of detail as possible. Utilities, telcos and finance companies fall into this category.

- The simple notion of good and bad customers separated only by their payment history is a gross over-simplification. The reality is closer to one where the majority of good customers are falling into process loops often caused by the company's failures. It is in the company's hands to make the relationships robust, and so avoid the customer having to interact with the business.

# Part IV
# Conclusions

# 11 Pulling it all together

## ABM COMES OF AGE

ABM's tentative beginnings were a response to the failure of traditional accounting practices to provide a solution to the problems of distortions arising in product costing. In particular, the increasing proportion of total costs represented by overhead costs in the manufacturing sector created the demand for a better analysis tool that would reflect the reality of how businesses actually worked.

Later, ABM approaches were extended to encompass product and customer profitability, which brought in the service sector, where costs associated with customers are a dominant proportion of the total. In many cases – for example, in the finance sector, distribution and the utilities – there have been few alternatives to ABM to provide a real understanding of the cost dynamics of their businesses. By extending the use of ABM data to give a process perspective on a business, the outputs from an ABM model provide the basis for initiating process improvements. Activity analysis, appropriately attributed to highlight the core activities that move the business forward and those activities put in place to deal with process failures, provides insights into how the business really works, and quantifies the opportunities for making improvements.

Performance measurement systems such as the Balanced Scorecard, the Business Excellence Model, Shareholder Value Added, and Positioning and Capability are all underpinned by using ABM analysis to provide a detailed understanding of where and how to take action to improve performance. ABM is not a passing fad, and neither is it a panacea to solve all business problems. ABM has come of age, and in the hands of able practitioners and enlightened management is an approach that creates essential information that can be acted on: actions that will make a real difference to business performance.

# ABM BRINGS A DIFFERENT PERSPECTIVE

ABM does not seek to displace and replace traditional accounting. Too much of tradition is now bound up in annual financial reporting required by legislation and the systems and procedures that collect data, rework it and feed it back to functional managers at monthly intervals. The key is to view ABM as an approach that makes essential information visible – information that leads to better decision-making on many levels. Every day, managers have to make decisions that must reduce the unit cost of processes, remove ineffective activities that add no value, predict the need for resources as business levels change, determine which products to make or services to provide, and which customers are good for the business and why. These are the decisions that lead to a profitable business: serving customers that it knows are valuable to retain.

But the key insight in ABM is to categorize costs in a way that reflects how the business actually works and the roles that managers have in either satisfying today's customers or securing a better future for the business. The traditional simple view of costs as either direct or overhead hides the rich diversity of the many tasks that are going on in organizations. ABM separates costs and activities into four categories: *infrastructure, sustaining, internal service,* and *frontline.* Viewing costs and activities in terms of these categories provides managers with a clear definition of their roles.

For those managers in the frontline, making today's products and servicing today's customers, their key role is to create robust processes at minimum unit costs so that the business can generate revenues significantly greater than the costs. The difference between revenues and costs, the ABM contribution, either at the product level or the customer level, is the basis for comparing the profitability of products and customers. It is this knowledge that determines the product port-folio and ideal customer mix.

The total ABM Customer Contribution provides the pot from which a pro-portion is invested in making a better future. These are the sustaining costs and activities. New products and services to the right customers secure a return on the investment of keeping sustaining costs in the business. Ensuring that this happens is the second key role of managers, a role that has an impact on the business over a longer timescale than today's frontline activities, but will create tomorrow's front-line costs and future contributions.

The relationship between frontline and sustaining is at the very heart of the business engine that is in place to ensure there is a business today and a better one in the future. Managers in the straitjacket of functional cost-centre reporting of the use of resources, tied up in the bonds of gross margin comparisons and blindfolded by the lack of process information, have little chance of seeing the engine, let alone the interaction of the vital components that ensure a reliable journey to a better future. ABM enables managers to see the engine, and to tune it with the right instrumentation.

## MAKING ABM HAPPEN

At an ABM seminar, delegates started the day with a number of concerns which, in summary, were as follows:

- Building an ABM model is very technical, and relies on manipulating complex software.
- An ABM project needs a lot of resources to make it happen. The organizational stress this creates just isn't worth it.
- ABM is the preserve of experts. You will never get managers in the business to use it to make a real difference to business performance.

The answers to these concerns are 'No', 'No' and 'No'. But there *is* a dilemma.

In the early days of ABM, the analysis of activities and activity drivers could be undertaken to any level of detail, but the analysis tools were unable to cope, so ABM models were crude, slow and cumbersome. As a result, the outputs from the model lacked credibility and risked not being acted upon. With the advent of sophisticated software tools and many more ABM experts, models of large size and great complexity can be built that contain fine detail and can calculate outputs in minutes rather than days. Vast outputs of data dumped regularly on managers' desks then have the same effect as the monthly management accounts out-turns. They are largely ignored: the sparkling gems of information are lost in the piles of sand. Planning ahead, relating the model's construction to the issues the model has to solve, keeping it simple, refreshing the model only when significant changes take place, presenting the model's outputs in a digestible form – all have a part to play in securing acceptance of the outputs by harassed managers.

But the key to a successful implementation is involvement and relevance. ABM has to start with both education and some serious listening to the issues that managers are facing. If managers cannot see the relevance of ABM to the business as a whole or to them in their everyday tasks, why should they spend precious time feeding yet another demand for information about how they and their people work? If an ABM project becomes an end in itself, stretching the capability and functionality of the software to the limit, operated by experts who speak another language that bears little resemblance to the real stuff of a line manager's day, then ABM becomes just another non-value-adding cost.

## ABM DOES MAKE A DIFFERENCE

ABM is now a flexible friend of many businesses and organizations, fully embedded into 'business as usual', a key support to management decision-making. Used appropriately, the blindfolds on the business are discarded. What is then seen sometimes shocks. Treasured products and a firm belief in retaining certain customers are now seen for what they are: a drain on profitability. The need for actions to enhance profitability may have lain hidden from view, but through ABM are now visible. People who have worked all their lives trapped behind the high walls of their functional fortresses now see to the horizon of customers via the multi-functional processes in which they work. People with long faces, spending every day on the treadmill of undertaking diversionary tasks that deal with process failures, now work with renewed energy on tasks which are core to taking the business forward.

There are many ways of spending a day. But if you prefer to spend time working on improving processes, determining which are profitable products for profitable customers, ensuring that you are spending the money that is made today on securing a better future, then today it is worth starting ABM.

# Appendix: Glossary of terms

**ABM Customer Contribution**    Revenue minus the product costs minus the costs of servicing the customer gives the ABM Customer Contribution. The sum of all the customer contributions has to pay for all those remaining costs that are not associated with the current products or customers, such as New Product Development and Statutory Accounting. Anything left after that is the profit. It is at the level of ABM Customer Contribution that we use the term 'customer profitability', as it is at this level that meaningful comparisons can be made between customers. This type of analysis exposes small or negative values, prompting a serious review of which customers to keep, or at least action to try to turn the relationship into one that provides positive contributions.

**ABM model**    A representation of resource costs during a time period that are consumed through activities and assigned to products, services and customers, or to any other object that creates a demand for the activity to be performed.

**ABM Product Contribution**    Revenue minus the real costs to produce the products based on an ABM analysis gives the ABM Product Contribution. It is at the level of ABM Product Contribution that we use the term 'product profitability', as it is at this level that meaningful comparisons can be made between products. This type of analysis exposes small or negative values, prompting a serious review of which products to keep, or at least action to try to turn them into positive contributions.

**activity**

Work performed by people, equipment, technologies or facilities. Activities may occur in a linked sequence (a process).

**activity analysis**

The process of identifying and cataloguing activities to enable detailed understanding and documentation of their characteristics. An activity analysis is accomplished by means of interviews, group sessions, questionnaires, observations, and reviews of physical records of work.

**Activity Based Budgeting (ABB)**

An approach to budgeting where a company uses an understanding of its activities and driver relationships to quantitatively estimate workload and resource requirements as part of an ongoing business plan. Budgets show the types, number of and cost of resources that activities are expected to consume, based on forecasted workloads.

**Activity Based Costing (ABC)**

A methodology that measures the cost and performance of cost objects, activities and resources. Cost objects consume activities, and activities consume resources. Resource costs are assigned to activities based on their use of those resources, and activity costs are reassigned to cost objects (outputs) based on the cost objects' proportional use of those activities. Activity-based costing incorporates causal relationships (cost drivers) between cost objects and activities, and between activities and resources.

212

**Activity Based Management (ABM)**

A discipline focusing on the management of activities within business processes as the route to continuously improve both the value received by customers and the profit earned in providing that value. ABM uses activity-based cost information and performance measurements to influence management action.

**activity dictionary**

A listing and description of activities that provides a common or standard definition of activities across the organization. An activity dictionary can include information about an activity and/or its relationships, such as activity description, business process, function source, inputs, outputs, supplier, customer, output measures, cost drivers, attributes, tasks, and other information as desired to describe the activity.

**activity driver**

The best single quantitative measure of the frequency and intensity of the demands placed on an activity by cost objects or other activities. It is used to assign activity costs to cost objects or to other activities.

**allocation**

A distribution of costs using calculations that may be unrelated to physical observations or direct or repeatable cause-and-effect relationships (for example, using Overhead Recovery Rates). Because of the arbitrary nature of allocations, costs based on cost driver analysis (as in ABM) are viewed as more relevant to management decision-making.

**assigning**

The practice of relating resources, activities and cost objects using the drivers underlying their cost causal relationships. The purpose of assigning is to observe and understand how costs are arising in the normal course of business operations.

**assignment**

A distribution of costs using causal relationships (cost drivers). Cost causal relationships are viewed as more relevant for management decision-making, and are the basis of ABM analysis approaches.

**attributes**

A label which provides additional classification or information about a resource, activity, or cost object. It is used to extract data from the model by the attribute. Attributes are used to define the process in which the activity takes place, a characteristic of the type of cost or work being done, or any other dimension which it is of interest to analyse.

**Balanced Scorecard**

A system of measurement and reporting to stakeholders other than the owners of the business, as well as in ways quite different to financial reporting. The Balanced Scorecard includes four perspectives. As well as the more traditional measures found in the financial perspective, the Scorecard includes customer, internal business, and learning perspectives.

**best practice**

A methodology that identifies the measurement or performance by which other similar items will be judged. This methodology is used to establish performance standards and to assist in identifying opportunities to increase effectiveness and efficiency. Best-practice methodology may be applied with respect to resources, activities, cost objects, or processes.

**budgetary accounting**

The tracking of costs to a budgetary account is often combined with cost-centre accounting. In this case, the major concern of the spenders of resources is to ensure that their total expenditures do not exceed the allocated budgetary amounts.

**Business Excellence Model**
A framework of measures developed by the European Foundation for Quality Management (EFQM). Like the Balanced Scorecard, the model takes a rounded view of an organization, using nine major dimensions of measurement.

**Business Process Management (BPM)**
A management approach that emphazises the process perspective rather than managing functions.

**Business Process Re-engineering (BPR)**
A method of analysing an organization from a process perspective that cuts through functional boundaries. A process is re-engineered to eliminate failures, waste or rework, or to enhance service levels. Manual activities may be displaced by automation or through the use of IT.

**CAM-I (Consortium for Advanced Manufacturing – International)**
This body researches all aspects of the manufacturing sector. CAM-I has been instrumental in promoting ABC as a superior approach for product costing.

**capability**
The sum of internal factors such as key business processes, procedures and systems, competencies, skills, education and training, attitudes, style and behaviours. Changing the capability of an organization enables it to change its positioning relative to other organizations.

**capacity**
The physical facilities, personnel and processes available to meet the product or service needs of customers. Capacity generally refers to the maximum output or producing ability of a machine, a person, a process, a factory, a product or a service.

**capacity management**
Management of the capacity of an organization at the level of machine, person, process, factory, product or service.

**constraint**

A bottleneck, obstacle or planned control that limits throughput or the utilization of capacity.

**core activities**

Activities that use specific skills and expertise and add real value to the business. Core activities are those that provide a necessary service to internal or external customers.

**cost centre**

A sub-unit in an organization that is responsible for costs.

**cost-centre accounting**

A method for applying resource costs to an organization. The accounting system identifies each of the organizational parts of the traditional functional structure, and applies the identifiable costs to that part of the structure.

**cost driver**

Any situation or event that causes a change in the consumption of a resource (resource driver) or activity (activity driver).

**cost driver analysis**

The examination, quantification and explanation of the effects of cost drivers. The results are often used for continuous improvement programmes to reduce throughput times, improve quality, and reduce cost.

**cost element**

The lowest-level component of a resource (item on the ledger).

**cost management**

The management and control of activities and drivers to calculate accurate product and service costs, improve business processes, eliminate waste, influence cost drivers, and plan operations. The resulting information can be used in setting and evaluating an organization's strategies.

**cost object**

Any product, service, customer, contract, project, process or other work unit for which a separate cost measurement is desired.

| | |
|---|---|
| **cost object driver** | The best single quantitative measure of the frequency and intensity of demands placed on a cost object by other cost objects. |
| **cost pool** | A logical grouping of resources or activities aggregated to simplify the assignment of resources to activities or activities to cost objects (for example, aggregating stationery consumables costs with salaries prior to assigning costs to activities to reduce the number of assignments in the model). |
| **cross-charges** | Cross-charges are used in an attempt to link services from one department to another, based on an estimate of the work done. However, as the underlying drivers of the activities are never the focus of a meaningful discussion between departments, cross-charges become an emotive issue and the source of much wasted argument. |
| **customer profitability** | *See* **ABM Customer Contribution**. |
| **Customer Relationship Management (CRM)** | The management of all aspects of the relationships with customers, though usually from the perspective of the information about customers – who they are, their attributes and behaviours, what they buy, and so forth – with a view to maximizing future sales of the right products to the right customers, and so engender long-term loyalty. |
| **direct assigned cost** | A cost that can be directly assigned to a cost object since a direct or repeatable cause-and-effect relationship exists. A direct assigned cost uses a direct assignment or cost causal relationship to transfer costs (for example, an external delivery charge). |
| **direct costs** | In a manufacturing business, direct costs are conventionally used to describe the raw materials that go into a product, and the labour content to manufacture piece parts and assemblies. |

217

**diversionary activities**

Activities caused by a process failure some-where in the organization which divert people away from their core activities. Such activities include correcting errors, chasing other groups for information, resolving queries and so forth. By re-engineering processes, diversionary activities are reduced or eliminated.

**Efficient Consumer Response (ECR)**

A term coined to encapsulate improving the chain that stretches from the basic raw material sources of a business through to the ultimate consumer. ECR has its foundation in the consumer products manufacturing and retailing sectors. ABM data provide an ideal information source to assist in the simulation of alternative ways of working and levels of service.

**embedding**

Constructing an ABM model starts the process of obtaining new benefits. Ensuring that the ABM approach is used in the longer term requires technical and management embed-ding. Technical embedding automates the links between the model and the organization's trans-action systems. Management embedding is the process of establishing ABM as a natural way of understanding the business and acting on the information ABM provides.

**enterprise-wide ABM**

A management information system that uses activity-based information to facilitate decision-making across an organization.

**European Foundation for Quality Management (EFQM)**

A grouping of European companies who spon-sored and developed the Business Excellence Model as a framework for measuring the effec-tiveness of an organization.

**frontline activity**

An activity that has something to do with pro-ducing the primary product or service and any activities that interface with customers. Front-line activities have a direct cause-and-effect relationship to products and customers through cost drivers.

**functional silos**

A term used to suggest that functions exist in virtual isolation with high walls around them.

**gross margin**

The gross margin is the difference between revenue and the direct costs. When this margin is positive, it is deemed to be making a contribution towards the costs of the overheads. However, an ABM analysis often shows that the real costs of the overheads for a particular product or customer are so high as to be greater than the gross margin. In these cases, increasing sales would erode profit, contrary to the indication from the gross margin, which would imply that more volume brings a greater contribution towards meeting overheads.

**hook curve**

A graph that plots cumulative profitability of either products or customers, starting with the highest profitability through to the lowest. When the lowest are negative, the curve has a characteristic 'hook' shape. The hook curve will generally show that the Pareto Rule holds true (that 80 per cent of the final profit comes from 20 per cent of the customers). However, the hook curve exposes another rule: that 125 per cent of the profit comes from 75 per cent of customers, the final 25 per cent of customers eroding the profit to the overall corporate figure.

**indirect assigned cost**

A resource or activity cost that cannot be assigned directly to a final cost object since no direct or repeatable cause-and-effect relationship exists.

**indirect costs**

In a manufacturing business, indirect costs are those activities, departments or functions that support the direct manufacturing activities,

219

such as the Quality department or Materials Handling.

**infrastructure costs**

Infrastructure costs exist because the organization is a legal entity and must fulfil specific tasks. The annual audit and financial reporting would fall into this category. Such costs are largely independent of the product or service being provided. They are the costs of being in business. These costs and activities have no causal relationships to current or future products and services. The level of such costs is unlikely to change with, say, throughput volumes or number of customers.

**internal service costs**

Typically, training, recruitment, and current use of IT networks are examples of internal services to all the other departments in the organization. There are no direct relationships to current products and customers other than through the frontline activities that are supported. The key here is to understand and then assign the internal service costs and activities in an appropriate manner to all the other areas of the business that are supported.

**ledger**

The ledger lists all the resources in an organization. The cost elements on the ledger are those things that provide the means so that work can be done in the organization. Cost elements would include salary costs for the people doing the work, accommodation costs so that people can work in buildings, utilities so that people can see what they are doing and keep warm, and vehicles so that goods can be delivered and customers visited. In some cases, the list of types of resource on the ledger may seem endless.

**life cycle cost**

A product's life cycle is the period that starts with the initial product conceptualization and ends with the withdrawal of the product from the marketplace and final disposition. A product life cycle is characterized by certain defined stages, including research, development, introduction, maturity, decline, and abandonment. Life cycle cost is made up of the accumulated costs incurred by a product during these stages.

**overhead costs**

All costs that are not defined as direct are overheads. The term 'overhead' is unhelpful as it lumps together a wide range of disparate costs and activities, all of which describe the rich diversity of the many functions in the business. The word 'overhead' and the American term 'burden' imply that overheads are in some way bad for the business. The key is to understand all the activities and how essential they are (or are not) to producing products and servicing customers. ABM very specifically analyses the overheads, and through causal relationships, links these costs to the products and services and onwards to customers.

**Pareto Analysis**

An analysis that compares cumulative percentages of the rank ordering of costs, cost drivers, profits or other attributes to determine whether a minority of elements have a disproportionate impact – for example, identifying that 20 per cent of a set of independent variables is responsible for 80 per cent of the effect.

**performance measures**

Indicators of the work performed and the results achieved in an activity, process, or organizational unit. Performance measures are both non-financial and financial. Performance measures enable periodic comparisons and benchmarking.

**positioning**

The sum of external factors such as understanding customer needs, understanding product and customer profitability, understanding

221

competitor initiatives, determining the business's financial needs, meeting changing legislation, and meeting environmental constraints.

**process**

A series of activities that are linked to complete a specific output.

**process mapping**

A powerful technique to track the cross-functional flow inside a business process. Such maps quickly highlight failure feedback loops and potential over-complication within a process. The emphasis needs to be on understanding the interaction between the people and the processes in which they work, particularly the points where the processes cross functional boundaries.

**product profitability**

*See* **ABM Product Contribution**.

**profitability analysis**

The analysis of profit derived from cost objects with a view to improving or optimizing profitability. Multiple views may be analysed, such as market segment, regions, distribution channel, customer segments, individual customers, product families, products and so forth.

**resource driver**

The best single quantitative measure of the frequency and intensity of demands placed on a resource by other resources, activities or cost objects. It is used to assign resource costs to activities and cost objects or to other resources.

**resources**

Cost elements applied or used in the performance of activities or to directly support cost objects. They include people, materials, supplies, equipment, technologies and facilities. Resources feature on the ledger.

**Shareholder Value Added (SVA)**

The net operating profit after tax minus the capital charge. The net operating profit after tax brings into focus prices, volumes, the cost of sales and all the operating expenses in the business, as well as taxes. The capital charge is all capital (net working capital plus net fixed capital) multiplied by the cost of capital.

**support activities**

Activities that make it possible for core activities to take place. For example, a salesperson's time spent negotiating with a customer is a core activity. The travelling time to get to the customer is support.

**surrogate cost driver**

A substitute for the ideal driver, but closely correlated to the ideal driver. A surrogate driver is used to significantly reduce the cost of measurement without significantly reducing accuracy.

**sustaining costs**

These costs are essentially an investment to achieve a return in the future. Organizations need to have funds to pay for the current costs of the people carrying out, say, new product development, but the benefits are expected to be derived in the future. The current product throughputs or current customers do not directly influence these activities. The organization has a choice over the level of sustaining costs it wants to have. A reduction in sustaining costs would transfer directly to the bottom line, but it would risk the future of the business. It could be argued that sustaining costs should be made specifically visible to shareholders, as they are investments in the business made out of retained profits that could have been distributed.

**target costing**

A target cost is calculated by subtracting a desired profit margin from an estimated or a market-based price to arrive at a desired production, engineering or marketing cost. This may not be the initial production cost, but one expected to be achieved during the mature production stage. Target costing is a method used in the analysis of product design that involves estimating a target cost and then designing the product/service to meet that cost.

**tasks**

The breakdown of the work in an activity into smaller elements.

**unit cost**

The cost associated with a single unit of measure underlying a resource, activity, product or service. It is calculated by dividing the total cost by the measured volume. Unit costs can be used for benchmarking or to construct models of new scenarios for running the business. Also used for Activity Based Budgeting.

**Value added (VA) and non-value added (NVA)**

Categories regularly used to separate out those activities that are good for the business from those that are not. From these categories, we would learn that creating scrap is bad, that checking is bad, and so forth. However, the terms VA and NVA are too coarse a definition of activities in the business, as the subtleties of how failures occur in processes and the impact of customer behaviours is largely invisible. (*See* **core**, **support** and **diversionary activities**)

**value analysis**

A method to determine how features of a product or service relate to cost, functionality, appeal and utility to a customer.

**Value Based Management (VBM)**

An approach to measuring the performance of a business, setting targets, finding and acting on the key value drivers that increase value, and embedding the continuous journey to higher value-creation through education and reward mechanisms. The key measure in VBM is Shareholder Value Added.

**value chain analysis**

A method to identify all the elements in the linkage of activities, starting from their point of origin, to manufacture and to distribute their products and services to an end user.

**value drivers**  The key variables that directly influence the creation of value in a business, such as price, volume, tax, operating expenses, cost of capital, fixed and working capital.

# Index

227

# Creating a Thinking Organization

## Groundrules for Success

Rikki Hunt with Tony Buzan

Imagine a company where staff have been taught to use their brainpower to the full - and are encouraged to do so whatever work they perform. In *Creating a Thinking Organization*, successful entrepreneur Rikki Hunt joins forces with renowned Mind expert Tony Buzan to provide a blueprint for individual and corporate transformation. Together they demonstrate how you can:

• unlock your own and your employees' potential;
• turbocharge your management and leadership practices, and
• motivate a diverse group of people.

Part I of the book explains how to apply Rikki Hunt's unique 'groundrules' to create a culture in which thinking will flourish. Part II looks at the nature of the human brain and describes a number of techniques to improve the thinking process. Part III, using Rikki's distinctive 'powerbase' and 'circles of knowledge' models, deals with leadership and examines the implications of the authors' approach both for the individual and the organization. Finally, Part IV contains practical guidance on implementation and summarizes the benefits. The text is enriched throughout by examples, stories, action point summaries, case studies and anecdotes from Rikki Hunt's own colourful life. In addition there are reviews of the material by Tony Buzan and a step-by-step development programme.

For business leaders seeking a way to harness the power of the brain, *Creating a Thinking Organization* will be an inspiration.

# Gower

# 50 Essential Management Techniques

Michael Ward

Are you familiar with the concept of product life-cycle? Of course you are! Does the prospect of a SWOT analysis bring you out in a cold sweat? Probably not. But what about the Johari Window? Or Zipf's Law?

Michael Ward's book brings together a formidable array of tools designed to improve managerial performance. For each entry he introduces the technique in question, explains how it works, then goes on to show, with the aid of an entertaining case study, how it can be used to solve an actual problem. The 50 techniques, including some never before published, are grouped into 11 subject areas, ranging from strategy to learning.

For managers in every type of organization and at any level, as well as for students and consultants, *50 Essential Management Techniques* is likely to become an indispensable source.

# Gower

# Ethics at Work

## Bob Kelley

Do you buy your raw materials where they're cheapest - even when they are produced by Third-World workers in conditions that would be illegal in your own country?

You're negotiating with a government department in a developing country: to secure the contract that will safeguard your company and your workforce, do you pay the customary 'commission' to the minister responsible?

When recruiting staff in Britain it isn't unlawful to discriminate on the grounds of religion - but is it right?

It's hardly possible to operate in the business world without encountering ethical dilemmas. Yet few companies pause to work out a set of policies and a way to apply them in its day-to-day dealings. In this timely book Bob Kelley identifies some of the underlying questions, explores possible answers and describes recent attempts to control corporate conduct.

Part I discusses ethical behaviour, including the attitudes found in various different cultures, and explains why the subject has risen so high up the current business agenda. Part II looks at the issues from the point of view of each of the five 'stakeholders' involved - owners, employees, customers, suppliers, and the community. Part III examines some of the methods used to regulate business, indicates some of the practical implications and speculates briefly about the future. The book concludes with a set of appendices containing the Nolan recommendations, the Institute of Management's guidelines, and details of relevant organizations.

Bob Kelley's book will be invaluable to every manager seeking guidance in this important and sensitive area.

# Gower

# The Excellent Manager's Companion

Philip Holden

This is for every manager who aspires to excellence in everything
they do, but wonders how they'll ever find the time ...

With *The Excellent Manager's Companion* in your desk drawer, you'll
be equipped with succinct guidance on today's most talked-about
business issues. And you'll be able to pepper your conversation
with pertinent quotations, and even know which books to turn to
when you really do need more detailed guidance on a specific topic.

Twenty-one chapters look at key topics, ranging from corporate
culture to customer orientation, and from innovation to
influencing people. Each chapter is organized around standard
sections, which makes 'dipping' into the book quick, easy,
and rewarding.

Sections are:

• questions for self-analysis
• a step-by-step guide to best practice
• the ten 'don'ts'
• pertinent quotations
• summaries of key books and articles
• a case study
• a glossary of terms.

Philip Holden's lively *Companion* combines expertise with
entertainment, with a supporting cast that ranges from Walt
Disney to Confucius, and from Dilbert to Drucker. This book is
guaranteed to appeal to busy managers in all sectors.

# Gower

# The Goal

## A Process of Ongoing Improvement Second Edition

Eliyahu M Goldratt and Jeff Cox

*A Gower Novel*

Written in a fast-paced thriller style, *The Goal* is the gripping novel which is transforming management thinking throughout the Western world. The author has been described by *Fortune* as 'a guru to industry' and by *Businessweek* as a 'genius'. It is a book to recommend to your friends in industry even to your bosses - but not to your competitors.

Alex Rogo is a harried plant manager working ever more desperately to try to improve performance. His factory is rapidly heading for disaster. So is his marriage. He has ninety days to save his plant - or it will be closed by corporate HQ, with hundreds of job losses. It takes a chance meeting with a colleague from student days - Jonah - to help him break out of conventional ways of thinking to see what needs to be done.

The story of Alex's fight to save his plant is more than compulsive reading. It contains a serious message for all managers in industry and explains the ideas which underlie the Theory of Constraints (TOC) developed by Eli Goldratt.

# Gower

# The Gower Handbook of Management

## Fourth Edition

### Edited by Dennis Lock

*'If you have only one management book on your shelf, this must be the one.'*

Dennis Lock recalls launching the first edition in 1983 with this aim in mind. It has remained the guiding principle behind subsequent editions, and today *The Gower Handbook of Management* is widely regarded as a manager's bible: an authoritative, gimmick-free and practical guide to best practice in management. By covering the broadest possible range of subjects, this *Handbook* replicates in book form a forum in which managers can meet experts from a range of professional disciplines.

The new edition features:

- 65 expert contributors - many of them practising managers and all of them recognized authorities in their field;
- many new contributors: over one-third are new to this edition;
- 72 chapters, of which half are completely new;
- 20 chapters on subjects new to this edition; and
- a brand new design and larger format.

*The Gower Handbook of Management* has received many plaudits during its distinguished career, summed up in the following review from *Director*:

*'... packed with information which can be used either as a reference work on a specific problem or as a guide to an entire operation. In a short review one can touch only lightly on the richness and excellence of this book, which well deserves a place on any executive bookshelf.'*

# Gower

# Gower Handbook of Management Skills

## Third Edition

Edited by Dorothy M Stewart

*'This is the book I wish I'd had in my desk drawer when I was first a manager. When you need the information, you'll find a chapter to help; no fancy models or useless theories. This is a practical book for real managers, aimed at helping you manage more effectively in the real world of business today. You'll find enough background information, but no overwhelming detail. This is material you can trust. It is tried and tested.'*

So writes Dorothy Stewart, describing in the Preface the unifying theme behind the Third Edition of this bestselling *Handbook*. This puts at your disposal the expertise of 25 specialists, each a recognized authority in their particular field. Together, this adds up to an impressive 'one stop library' for the manager determined to make a mark.

Chapters are organized within three parts: Managing Yourself, Managing Other People, and Managing the Business. Part I deals with personal skills and includes chapters on self-development and information technology. Part II covers people skills such as listening, influencing and communication. Part III looks at finance, project management, decision-making, negotiating and creativity. A total of 12 chapters are completely new, and the rest have been rigorously updated to fully reflect the rapidly changing world in which we work.

Each chapter focuses on detailed practical guidance, and ends with a checklist of key points and suggestions for further reading.

# Gower

# How to Make Work FUN!

## An Alphabet of Possibilities ...

David Firth

With the majority of our lives spent either at work or asleep it seems crazy to consign 'fun' only to life outside of the office. Why do we leave our personalities behind when we set off for work in the morning? Why do we envy people who tell us that their work is fun, yet somehow feel laughter is out of place in the office? And how can we deliver excellent service, or be better than our competitors, if we'd rather not be working at all?

This book is a must for anyone who'd like to foster a team spirited positive working environment, get work into perspective (reduce stress levels), or simply enjoy work more. It should be studiously avoided by anyone who feels threatened by the very idea of deriving fun from work.

# Gower

# Mind Skills for Managers

Samuel A Malone

How good are you at managing multiple tasks? What about problem solving and creativity? How quickly do you pick up new ideas and new skills?

Managers are measured against some tough criteria. You may feel that you're already doing everything that you can, and you're still being asked for more. But in one area you've got over 90% of unused capacity ... your brain.

*Mind Skills for Managers* will help you to harness your mind's unused capacity to:

• develop your ability to learn
• generate creative ideas
• handle information more effectively
• and tackle many of the key skills of management in new and imaginative ways.

Sam Malone mixes down-to-earth ideas with techniques such as Mind Maps, checklists, step-by-step rules, acronyms and mnemonics to provide an entertaining, easy-to-use guide to improving your management techniques by unleashing the full power of your mind.

The skills in this book need to be practised. The best approach is to take one idea at a time and apply it. By following the book you will learn a whole range of 'mind skills' and be rewarded by measurable improvements in your performance.

Use and implement the ideas and you will think better, think faster and work smarter.

Gower

# The New Time Manager

Angela V Woodhull

Why is it that, when there are exactly 168 hours in everyone's week, some people accomplish so much more than others? Often they're the same people who appear least stressed and enjoy both personal and professional lives the most.

Dr Woodhull's absorbing book explains the key principles of modern time management and shows how to apply them in our day-to-day activities. Traditional time management revolved mainly around to-do lists and delegating. *The New Time Manager* is concerned far more with factors like developing good working relationships and establishing a healthy lifestyle. For example, New Time Managers:

• prioritize
• communicate effectively
• give constructive feedback
• take time to play
• act to prevent burnout.

The result is a life in balance, with sufficient time for what is important to you. Whatever your objective, Dr Woodhull's book, with its practical guidance on every aspect of time, will help you.

# Gower

# The Ultimate How To Book

## Strategies for Personal Achievement

Harry Alder

There seems no end to the stream of 'How to' books pouring out of the world's printing presses. This one, though, is different. You might even call it the key to all the others. Most 'How to' books promise some specific outcome, for example fluent Spanish, or a six-figure income. But without the right sort of self-beliefs, success will be hard to achieve. Dr Alder deals with that process of achievement. He shows how, by mastering a few simple strategies, you can:

• make the most of that amazingly powerful machine, the human brain
• use goal-setting to increase your chances of success
• motivate yourself by controlling your state of mind
• harness your natural creativity
• turn obstacles into opportunities.

What *The Ultimate How To Book* offers is nothing less than a technology of personal achievement. With its help you can get whatever you want to get, do whatever you want to do, be whatever you want to be.

Gower